Endorseme

When I first met Emma, it was almost 15 years ago. I was a young man then. She came into a church in Aberdeen, Scotland, owned by a mutual late mentor of ours, Bishop Joe Ibojie. With a blonde bob-cut hairdo and a stylish jacket, she sat down at the table that Dr. Sharon Stone and I were talking at. Her first words were, "Hi, Sharon. I've just come back from dealing with these Freemason spirits and they're awful...." As she continued her dialogue, the single greatest thought running through my head was, *Who is this woman?* She progressed to speak about how a demon-oppressed Freemason had somehow managed to get onto the roof of a building! I stared and stared, wondering as to the peculiarity of her accent mixed with this Irish/Scottish gusto that could only be described as Mel Gibson from *Braveheart*.

She ended her dialogue with, "And who's this?" Suddenly, I was forced to break out of my trance and pretend that I wasn't winded by her absolute audaciousness. I said, "Er, hi, er, I'm Tomi!" I had no wild Freemason-demon-busting story to impress this now profoundly prophetic table with, and my only contribution was simply as a silent listener. I've been listening ever since.

Emma has been such a bastion for the prophetic movement. Her passion to see prophets raised up has separated her from the average crop of prophets (if there be such a thing as "average" among the prophets). What sets Emma above the rest is her marriage. I have watched her raise her three children to be avid prophetic voices and God-fearing, wonderful human beings. I have watched her love and honor her husband and model what a global prophetic ministry with a wholesome marriage can achieve. Whilst many of my colleagues have started a ministry and ended a marriage, Emma is what we Brits like to call a WYSIWYG: "What You See Is What You Get!"

What I admire most about Emma is that her ability to reproduce prophets has always started in her home. What you and I now see as a successful, thriving ministry is just the upscale of her lifestyle. I'm honored to know her and her family. I truly hope this book blesses and releases many more prophets so needed in the earth today.

Tomi Arayomi
Tomi Arayomi Ministries
Founder, Rig Nation

The Holy Spirit promises us not only a global outpouring of His presence, power, and gifting, but also, according to Acts 3:19-21, that there will be a "restoration of all things spoken by the holy prophets of old." We need more than just the restoration of the gifts of the Spirit, we need a restoration of relevant methods of delivery, an understanding of proper protocol and stewardship, and the restoration of the glorious promise in our prophetic message. Not only that, but in reality, we need the Holy Spirit to bring a healing, cleansing, and greater wholeness to individual prophetic messengers and to the global prophetic movement as a part of this end-time global movement of restoration. In my Destiny Image book, *The Prophet: Creating a Life-Giving Prophetic Culture*, I made an attempt to speak into these things. Now, Emma Stark picks up the baton with her next-generation style on *Becoming the Voice of God*. You see, it is not enough to just hear the voice of God; we are mandated to become what we hear. It is time for Incarnational Authentic Prophetic Christianity!

DR. JAMES W. GOLL
Founder of God Encounters Ministries
Author, Singer, and Creative Consultant

Emma Stark is not passive. She is not someone who is satisfied to dwell in the status quo or to operate within the mediocre. Emma Stark is a stirrer, an agitator, and a provoker. She is these things because she is a prophet and because she is a reformer. Her heart is to see the Bride make herself ready for Christ's return. Her desire is to see maturity come forth in the body of Christ. This book is a manifestation of her walk and the lessons that she has learned in the process.

As I look at the modern church, I see many prophetic people but not many prophets. *Becoming the Voice of God* seeks to address this. It is not a book for pastors. In fact, those with a pastoral anointing should probably not read this book. It is a book that seeks to shift the prophetic movement out of yesterday and into tomorrow. This book is not a "how-to guide to prophesy," or "a beginner's guide to the prophetic." It is a challenge to the prophetic movement to mature and enter a whole new wave in God. It is calling forth the prophets and explaining what is required of them. It is summoning folks out of their gifting and into their calling. It is setting the agenda for the role of the prophet for at least the next 20 years! This book is a whetstone for a blunt prophetic movement.

PHIL SANDERSON
Senior Pastor, River Church Aberdeen, UK
Core Leader, British Isles Council of Prophets

Emma is a gift to the church as she courageously and passionately calls the body of Christ to make room for the prophets. This book is a beacon—it gives hope for the prophets and for the future of the church. It is full of wisdom and insights to help you understand the leadership that prophets are called to bring to the church. Read it if you sense God has gifted you as a prophet. Read it if you are a church leader working out how to receive the ministry of prophets. This book caused me to repent, intercede, and long for a church that is humble enough to leave behind mindsets and practices that have denied the role of prophets. This is an invitation to be a church that is shaped by the life and culture of heaven under the Lordship of Jesus, and for that to happen, we need the prophets.

REV. CANON JOHN MCGINLEY
Leader of the Myriad Church
Planting Ministry, London, England

It is a joy for my wife Joe and me to count the Starks as our dearest friends. We have walked together now for more than two decades. Over this time, it has been my joy to minister both nationally and internationally with Emma, and I've seen her truly become God's voice on the earth. Emma is a true prophet, and I can think of no one more qualified to write a book on the office of the prophet.

You hold in your hands a masterpiece that will equip you, shake you, challenge you, and pull you up into your true identity and calling. The contents of this book come out of years of experience, both from ministering as a prophet and also raising up and equipping others to do so. *Becoming the Voice of God* is far more than a book, it is a spiritual encounter: a commissioning and a prophetic declaration of the birthing fresh prophetic movement in the earth.

Becoming the Voice of God is sure to become essential reading and a spiritual classic for those seeking to go deeper into the high calling of the New Testament prophet. I highly recommend this book.

Simon Braker
Legacy Ministries International
Core Leader, British Isles Council of Prophets

Many years ago, while ministering in Scotland, I called out a beautiful young woman and declared over her that she was a prophet. That woman was Emma Stark. She received that word and ran with it 100 percent. Today Emma is still known for her full trust in whatever God tells her, courageous encounters with God, and authority to prophetically drive out devils. She is a spiritual pioneer who causes others to be pulled into greater divine revelation. This book is a testament to her forerunning.

Dr. Sharon Stone
Founder, Prophetic Voice

When God wants to change a culture, the church, or a nation, He always raises up prophets. With *Becoming the Voice of God,* Emma Stark has written a very important book for our times. It challenges many of the mindsets and doctrines that have limited the functioning of those called to the prophetic office. It also lays a framework for the emergence of a righteous prophetic company that is free from the fear of man. I have known Emma Stark for years now. Her boldness inspires many in Europe—and around the world—to fearlessly proclaim the prophetic word of God. She is a great prophet and a good friend. I highly recommend this book.

Dr. Arleen Westerhof
Co-Director, European Prophetic Council
Co-Lead Pastor, God's Embassy Amsterdam

Five years ago, when I first met Emma, our mutual passion to see the next generation of prophets in Europe recognized and trained connected us immediately. Emma Stark is probably Europe's leading prophet for this hour, and her brilliant new book will catapult the church into a much-needed practical and sound understanding of how and why we need established prophets so urgently today.

PERNILLE LILAND
Leader, Nordic Prophetic Network & Roundtable of Prophets

Emma Stark's new book *Becoming the Voice of God* is a brilliant and practical manual that gives a theologically sound perspective on the role and lifestyle of the prophet. It shares insightful truths regarding the development of prophets, the importance of their call, and how they can be effective in ministry. Emma writes from years of wisdom and experience as she has led a thriving prophetic movement. This book is inspiring, challenging, and thought-provoking, and is a must-read for every believer.

BRENDAN and SHARON WITTON
Lead Pastors, Toronto City Church, Canada

The first time I heard Emma speak, I realized I was hearing the sound and voice of a new generation of prophets. It was pristine, it was sharp, it was strong, and it was from Heaven. I was deeply stirred and awakened and that's what prophets do; they awaken us to the realities of the unseen. I fully endorse Emma Stark and what God has placed in her.

REV. YANG TUCK YOONG
Senior Pastor, Cornerstone Community Church, Singapore
Director, The Bible College of Wales, Swansea

This book contains key insights into the maturing of the prophetic movement at this time in God's church. It contains biblical rootedness and practical wisdom in unpacking the role of a prophet today. It will serve both those called by God to be a prophet and those called by God to work with prophets, creating the space for them to flourish and be the gift they're meant to be within a healthy community, fivefold team ministry, and a culture of honor. It felt like something of a road map to me for the next few years as the prophets see and speak out the necessary dismantling of cultures and structures that no longer serve God's purposes. Then, together with apostolic leaders, we can build new shapes, cultures, and pioneering models that prepare the church to be able to handle a greater outpouring of His Spirit, bring transformation, and, ultimately, become a radiant bride for King Jesus.

Ness Wilson
Leader, Pioneer UK

Emma Stark is a passionate, courageous prophet—relentless in her pursuit of God, His Word, and His Spirit! This groundbreaking and thought-provoking work is essential reading to understand the second wave of the prophetic movement that is now upon us. With a rich blend of biblical weight and prophetic insight, Emma clearly lays out the call and role of the prophet today—prophets with maturity, with power, with "teeth"—a true representation of the fullness of God's character and a pure echo of His voice in the earth. You'll be challenged and inspired by the life-changing prayers and activations and humbled by the invitation to take your seat in the council of God!

Louise Reid
Leader, Ireland Council of Prophets
Core Leader, British Isles Council of Prophets

Whenever Emma Stark enters a room, the atmosphere shifts. It's not just her incredible outfits or personal charisma: this is a woman who carries an authority in the Spirit that rattles, rocks, and rolls principalities and powers and shakes awake believers. Emma raises the stakes and raises the standard everywhere that she goes. She is a walking shot of espresso to the soul and spirit. Her boldness electrifies. She is also one of the most generous and fun people I know.

In these intense days of radical God-led reform inside the worldwide church, God has raised bold champions like Emma to provoke and equip us for the new. The fear of the Lord is all over this book. *Becoming the Voice of God* has challenged me, humbled me, and continues to both daunt and inspire me. Read it with awe and trembling and let the Spirit of God get ahold of you.

Adele Richards
Senior Leader, Catch the Fire Church, Bournemouth, UK
Core Leader, British Isles Council of Prophets

In her book, *Becoming the Voice of God*, Emma Stark states that "prophets are a grit in the oyster of the people of God. They comfort the afflicted and afflict the comfortable!" I have known Emma as a friend and prophet for many years and would say that's true of Emma herself. I've seen her be the grit, drawing out the pearl of prophetic unction and ministry in many people's lives. Emma carries a recognized mandate as a trainer and equipper in the prophetic community. Emma's passion and gifting stand as a strong beacon, providing illumination and understanding in navigating prophecy.

Emma's new book offers an insight into the prophetic with truths infused with hard-won wisdom and experience. If you're looking to invest in growing your gifting and a new way of seeing and working within the prophetic, this book, written to captivate a new generation of readers, is the book for you.

PREETHY KURIAN
Founder, Capstone Church, London
London Prophetic Centre
British Isles Council of Prophets

Want to discern if you are a prophet? Buckle up, because this book will take you on a biblical journey where the voice of God will no longer just come forth from others but will now bubble up and flow through you! Emma Stark is a servant of the Lord who holds the fivefold ministry gift in the office of the prophet. She hears and discerns the voice of God with accuracy and power. This book demonstrates her desire and strong biblical conviction to raise up and call forth the voice of God in other believers. As pastors in DC, we have been challenged through Emma's teachings to become the voice of God in our church and nation.

AARON and AMY GRAHAM
Lead Pastors, The District Church, Washington DC

God is looking for your authentic voice, courage, and boldness to stand out. It is time for the prophetic voice in you to arise, come forth, come out, speak, and prophesy. As you are becoming the voice of God, you need wisdom and insight not to find yourself stuck or stagnant. This book carries a message to encourage you to keep looking and pursuing to be the original voice God has called you to be. At the same time, it pushes you to the edge of your seat to walk the road less traveled. Emma brilliantly teaches you how to steward revelation with both responsibility and accountability.

Prophet, arise and come up higher. We feel that the weight and importance of the prophetic ministry is rising, and the prophets need to get prepared and ready. These blueprints from

Emma help you gain years of insight from personal experience given in the battle trenches by simply reading a book. The reward of the prophet is a word, and here the word invites you to step deeper than the shallow waters; it teaches you to be sharp and how to deliver your prophecy with structure and authority. May we become revolutionary, wild, radical, and biblical stewards of the mysteries of God.

Read it, and then read it again!

BJARKI CLAUSEN
I AM Equipping Center, Iceland

My dear friend Emma has done it again. Another cutting-edge, must-read reference book for prophets of today to consume and learn from.

As fivefold ministers, we have faithfully stood on the shoulders of our mothers and fathers to carry the fire and equip an army fit for purpose. In *Becoming the Voice of God*, Emma takes us further into God's intention for the second-wave prophetic movement. She shares her own life story as an example of one who has said "yes" to the call as a prophet, one who is wholly committed to raising a mature prophetic army that will be effective ministers in the new era. With theological understanding and prophetic insight, Emma challenges the status quo and leads us courageously into uncharted territory to forge a new path, moving from institution to a revolution of our mindset and prophetic function. Her penetrating look into the history of the prophetic movement and the timely prophetic insight for our future will challenge the comfortable and spur the reader on to embrace their high call to courageous prophetic ministry.

LYNLEY ALLAN
Senior Leader, Catch the Fire Auckland

New Zealand Prophetic Council

The prophet's voice is a necessity if we want to enter the fullness of all that God intends for our cities and our nations. This book comes at a time in history where there is a cry to see the emerging prophets rise up and walk in partnership within the fivefold in a healthy way. Emma writes with a biblically sound yet firm grasp of the prophet's mandate. The purpose of this book is to train emerging prophets worldwide to establish His Kingdom on earth.

JOËL and HANNAH DUMAINE
Génération Unité, Canada

DESTINY IMAGE BOOKS BY EMMA STARK

Lion Bites

The Prophetic Warrior

Freedom from Fear

BECOMING THE
VOICE
OF GOD

NEXT-LEVEL TRAINING
FOR PROPHETIC PEOPLE

EMMA STARK

Dedication

For the prophets I have taught; for the prophets I have mentored; for the prophets who have sharpened me; for the prophets ready to listen — this is for you.

But mostly, this is for my children—Jessica, Peter, and Samuel. May you be free to be all that God has called you to be and remain at the cutting edge of His purposes on the earth.

For my husband, David, who has bravely championed and loved me so deeply—it has enabled me to step into the wild things of God.

DESTINY IMAGE® PUBLISHERS, INC.
P.O. Box 310, Shippensburg, PA 17257-0310
"Publishing cutting-edge prophetic resources to supernaturally empower the body of Christ"

This book and all other Destiny Image and Destiny Image Fiction books are available at Christian bookstores and distributors worldwide.

For more information on foreign distributors, call 717-532-3040.
Reach us on the Internet: www.destinyimage.com.

ISBN 13 TP: 978-0-7684-6260-9
ISBN 13 eBook: 978-0-7684-6261-6

For Worldwide Distribution, Printed in the U.S.A.
2 3 4 5 6 7 8 / 27 26 25 24

CONTENTS

FOREWORD

SEVERAL YEARS AGO, I was ministering to a group of well-known leaders and students who had gone through supernatural and prophetic training from a very popular Charismatic movement. While I was preaching, I had a strange spiritual experience where I was shown an assignment from the devil against a particular leader and his wife. I outlined three specific attacks that their marriage would face over the next seven years and assured them of victory as God gave them clear direction of hope in the midst of trial through the prophetic word. I have never felt the love of God for a particular couple like I did that night.

After the meeting, the couple in leadership that I had prophesied over came up to me and said that they renounced everything I said to them because it wasn't positive enough. They said their prophetic and supernatural training had instructed them to not receive any negative words. Sadly, this couple was divorced within that same year. Isn't it amazing that I was personally encountering the love of God for that couple as I prophesied to them because He was so kind to warn and expose them to the devil's plans ahead of time, yet they failed to receive it because it wasn't "positive" enough.

With so much global confusion surrounding the modern-day ministry of prophets, I found this book both refreshing and carrying a realm of clarity that is desperately needed in the body of Christ. This precious manuscript needs to be read in every local church and prophetic training center around the world. Emma Stark is a firebrand who has been anointed for this hour. The prophetic ministry God has given her speaks for itself, and her ability to pen present-day truth from heaven is remarkable.

I have personally served what God has called her to build in Scotland and found it built upon the Word of God and the Voice of God. Her marriage and family are healthy and she truly lives what she preaches. We have hosted her at our church in North Carolina, and I have ministered alongside of her around the world. The authority, humility, and purity she carries is both evident and contagious. May this book help to multiply the God-breathed DNA of Emma Stark like never before!

Receiving the capacity as prophets of God to minister prophetic words that correct, rebuke, uproot, and tear down is no small matter in the sight of God. In fact, this calling is so sacred to the heart of God that it becomes much easier to recognize who has a true calling to be a prophet and who does not by how these types of words are delivered to people. Mature prophets of God will never deliver weighty and corrective words of prophecy without agony and at times with much weeping and prayer. A true prophet will continually find him/herself caught in the tension of standing before a holy God and yet called to minister to sinful man. Authentic prophets cringe at, but must embrace, their assignment at times to turn the people back to God through cries for repentance, holiness, and returning to first love.

Those in the body of Christ who have been given the gift of prophecy have limitations placed upon them per 1 Corinthians 14. The prophetic words they deliver must be full of encouragement, comfort, and strength. However, and as mentioned above, true prophets will not only follow the guidelines mentioned in

1 Corinthians 14 but they have also been given permission and capacity to confront, rebuke, expose, and uproot when necessary (see Jeremiah 1; Revelation 2, 3).

Will prophets continually and always move in this capacity? Absolutely not! In fact, if prophets only confront and rebuke and never build up and plant, they are unbalanced and dangerous. New Testament prophets operate in a healthy prophetic anointing when they edify, exhort, and comfort, but they may also at times challenge and expose demonic practices, doctrinal error, and false prophets who endorse unbiblical standards not found in the Word of God.

Please read each chapter of this book more than once. Let the prophetic clarity that Emma carries overcome the confusion and political correctness surrounding modern-day prophetic ministry. Commit to get into the place of prayer and the Word of God like never before. There is a deeper encounter with Jesus the prophet waiting for you and Emma Stark has brilliantly lit the path for you to find your way there. Our best days in the prophetic are still ahead of us. The need for a clarion call, like this book gives, has never been greater!

JEREMIAH JOHNSON
Founder of the Altar Global Movement
Author of *The Warrior Bride*

INTRODUCTION

SOME YEARS AGO, I was sitting with my eyes closed in a prayer meeting. Suddenly, a bellowing voice trumpeted overhead, "Emma, you do not only have a prophetic gift; you have a prophetic office. Come into that office." I felt the burning weight of God in the words but had utterly no idea what they meant or how they would completely redefine my life. Opening my eyes and looking up in the room where I was, I saw my leader almost pass out with the presence of God as she commissioned me in the Spirit, and before men, to be a prophet.

My first thought was, "Jesus, help!" This was quickly followed by a flood of questions like, "Where can I go for assistance?" and "Who knows about being a prophet?" The quality options available to me, I soon discovered, were very limited!

My life up to this pivotal point had been well punctuated with visions, dreams, and hearing God, but I knew that now He was requiring something weightier from me. He wanted words to come out of my mouth that would shape lives, demolish demonic strongholds, and truly establish His Kingdom. I needed help!

The contemporary prophetic movement is relatively young. With its founding father Dr. Bill Hamon still being alive, we can only count its age in decades rather than in centuries. On the other hand, for the last few hundred years if you wanted to become a church teacher or a pastor, there would have been a plethora of Bible college and seminary options to choose from. But where would you have gone to become a prophet and how do you become the voice of God? The modern-day giants in the prophetic movement such as Bishop Hamon and his family, Cindy Jacobs, James Goll, John Paul Jackson, Patricia King, Bobby Conner and others were, in the purest form, pioneers, blazing into virgin territory for the church. Even some foundational prophetic concepts and conventions that we would find commonplace today only became established in recent years. For example, the familiar sight of a prophet prophesying over people in a line, delivering word after word as people wait with their cassette tapes to record, was only developed in the lifetime of these trailblazers—in other words, the realization that we could prophesy on demand is relatively new. Of course, we have written prophecies by key individuals from across the whole life span of the church, but we have very little in the way of a highly active legacy, succession planning, raising up, and establishing of a prophetic church and a prophetic movement across the world. This is about to change, and you are part of it.

We still collectively wrestle with concepts and questions such as: When and if you should repent if a prophecy doesn't come to pass? What constitutes a false prophet? What role does the prophet have in the church and the nation? Should a prophet speak into nations that they don't live in—and what are their lines of authority? How much should they be forth-telling about the future? Who judges a prophet's words? What is the balance between prophesying with the wrath and judgment of God versus His love and mercy? And is there a difference between an Old Testament and a New Testament prophet?

It is time that we settle some of these questions and make their answers foundation stones under our feet, so that you and I might now get on with the business of reformation and transformation in nations and the building of a revelatory church. Most prophetic people I have trained over many years suffer terribly from so-called "impostor syndrome," continually wrestling with whether they are a spokesperson for God or not. The orphan spirit looms large over prophetic people, so much so that they often feel they must prove they can prophesy by overstating what they are hearing and thus putting us all off by their odd extremes, or by prophesying only in exaggerated tones about wealth, promotion, and breakthrough in order to persuade people to accept and like them. You could almost play catchphrase bingo at most prophetic conferences, knowing that you will repeatedly hear things like, "You will advance!" "Things are accelerating for you!" "This is the moment of your breakthrough!" "God just wants you to know you are loved," or, "It's a new day." Many over-familiar words like this can feel shallow. After all, most of today's so-called "prophets" are not prone to saying, "You are in a process," "You're not going to like the season you're in," or, "God is disciplining you!"

PRAYER

I decree in the name of Jesus Christ that the orphan spirit, rejection, and imposter syndrome comes off you right at the start of walking through this book with me. I pray that you might right now begin to step into the fullness of your call. In the name of Jesus, I release over you the ability to accept and receive what God has spoken into life—that you are to be His voice for many. Agree with me for the removal of all imposter tendencies and reject out loud any sense you have of unworthiness to be a voice for God. We are all in places of unmerited favor and undeserved grace.

While we *do* have a glorious array of mature prophet leaders, the entire prophetic movement is still shifting from adolescence to adulthood in how it stewards the word of God.

We are all stepping up into a new day in the prophetic movement. I want to grab hold of your hand and take you on a journey to stretch you and to muse together with you about what God is doing with the prophetic movement. Most of all, my job in this book is to very practically assist you to become the voice of God and to become what you know you should be, as God pulls a new identity out of you. As He exposes the richness of revelation that He has set inside you, let us adventure together so that you might portray who you really are, anywhere that you find yourself. So please walk with me as we wrestle the hot issues within the modern-day prophetic movement and search the Scriptures, that we may become a *mature* prophetic church.

> The entire prophetic movement is still shifting from adolescence to adulthood in how it stewards the word of God.

EMERGING AS A PROPHET

It is the folly of too many to mistake the echo of a London coffee-house for the voice of the kingdom.

—Jonathan Swift
Irish author of *Gulliver's Travels* and
Dean of St. Patrick's Cathedral, Dublin

CHAPTER 1

WHAT IS A PROPHET?

LET'S TALK ABOUT the office of the prophet! "Office" is a way of saying "role" or "position." The Bible records that God spoke once through a bush, once through a donkey, and 54 times through angels. But there are 769 instances when God spoke through a prophet in Scripture. There is a total of:

- 1,817 prophecies and
- 8,352 verses of prophecy in the Bible.
- Approximately 27 percent of Scripture is prophecy.

Is 27 percent of our church life prophecy? Are prophetic words underpinning the vision and direction of *your* church in the way that they did for the people of God in Scripture? Fifteen of the books in the Old Testament were written by prophets, the big three being those of Ezekiel, Isaiah, and Jeremiah. Jeremiah is the longest book in the Bible by word count, and the total words in the books of the prophets equals those in the whole of the New Testament!

Prophets are seen from Genesis to Revelation and, as we walk the story of Scripture, the words of the prophets hold leaders and nations accountable, they set timings, and they give direction, correction, and solution on almost every page.

Prophets are the strangest of our biblical characters. On occasions we find them prophesying naked and hiding their underwear behind a rock—and then putting it back on when it is full of holes—to show the lack of intimacy the people had with their God. They waft down mountainsides, shadowing kings and bringing them into their right mind. Some crunch insects for breakfast and others marry prostitutes. They stage plays with horned helmets, acting out battle scenes to make a point. They weave elaborate stories to bring kings to repentance. One even kills—with his own hands—850 false prophets in a single day, in what would have been a bloodbath victory. Prophets mistakenly think they are alone—which becomes one of their Achilles' heels and a false reality that haunts prophetic people to this day, when in fact the truth is that God always has some other prophets hiding away nearby. If *you* think that you are alone and that nobody understands you, it is more likely a sign that you have not understood your biblical mandate to replicate and pull up others into their call (more on this later). Isolated prophets are dangerous prophets!

> Prophets are the grit in the oyster of the people of God. They comfort the afflicted and afflict the comfortable!

Prophets are bold, confrontational, often irritating, annoying, marginalized—and even killed—and they prefer if things happen immediately. They are the grit in the oyster of the people of God. They comfort the afflicted and afflict the comfortable.

There are eighty-five prophets named in the Bible. Sixty are found in the Old Testament and twenty-five in the New. Many more are alluded to but not named in the schools and companies of prophets led by the likes of Elijah and Samuel. There are nine women in the Bible who are prophets: Miriam (Exodus 15:20), Deborah (Judges 4:4), Huldah (2 Kings 22:14), Isaiah's wife (Isaiah 8:3), Anna (Luke 2:36-38), and the four daughters of Philip (Acts 21:8-9).

Many more speak prophetically, such as Rachel (Genesis 30:24), Hannah (1 Samuel 2:1-10), Abigail (1 Samuel 25:28-31), Elizabeth (Luke 1:41-45), Mary the mother of Jesus (Luke 1:46-55), along with Sarai/Sarah and Esther.

And of course, there is a good smattering of false prophets who show how it should *not* be done and must serve as a good warning to us so that we do not inadvertently become their disciples.

Joyously, the prophet is not a dying or dead breed! Neither are prophets to be a rare spectacle, for Joel promises us an increase in both men and women who can be the voice of God as we come close to end times:

> *I will pour out my Spirit on all people. Your sons and daughters will prophesy, your old men will dream dreams, your young men will see visions. Even on my servants, both men and women, I will pour out my Spirit in those days* (Joel 2:28-29 NIV).

Perhaps one of the most striking foretelling New Testament passages is found in Revelation 11, where an entire type of church arises—a prophetic church with specific prophets who are raised up to speak in the latter days, modeled on Moses and Elijah, and who will bring words with fire in their mouths. They will catalyze a renewal of worship. It is a reemergence of prophets who command weather, speak plagues into being, devour enemies, and give true testimony to Jesus. We are entering the days of becoming the Revelation 11 church, where the remnant (that's you!) will have a God-given and God-protected vocation to be faithful, purified prophets. Satan is terrified of this kind of divinely authorized prophetic ministry.

> We are entering the days of becoming the Revelation 11 church, where the remnant will have a God-given and God-protected vocation to be faithful, purified prophets.

PROPHETIC WORD: YOU ARE BECOMING THE REVELATION 11 PEOPLE

Let me prophesy. The Spirit of the Lord says:

> I will dress the prophets in clean garments; they will rebuke satan. You shall receive a most mighty gift—that of living, seeing, receiving, and becoming the Revelation 11 people. You shall not be like the people who went before you, who did not live long enough to see promise fulfilled. But you shall live, and I will require you to become the Revelation 11 people. My church will be a prophetic church, my church will have a prophetic vocation. You will only be blessed to proceed into the new era if you will create change by revelation. No longer will the church live out of human reasoning. You will hear things, see things, and spiritually

process all of your decisions. The prophetic church is activated today! The prophetic will become the key that opens the door to this new age.

You will build by revelation. The prophets will live by revelation rather than speak revelation only or echo others' revelation. You will not make decisions by borrowing another's prophecy, and I will not bless you to take another's words as your own. Neither will you live by a franchise model—for this is the day of My revelatory people who know what I say specifically to their nation, their region, their church, and their family. You will watch people fail fast when they marry another person's revelation and covenant with what I said to someone else and not them.

How you start to build will set the trajectory for the rest of your lives, as My prophetic people create prototypes that will be built by revelation. Even new technology will come from My people. Prototypes will come forth from you and a creative river will gush forth from you.

Prayer

As I pray for you now, physically position yourself to receive from God:

In the name of Jesus, I loose an ability for you to grow and become established in revelation and for you to live by the Spirit and by the voice of God. Amen.

The Prophet's Role

As we journey from Genesis to Revelation, we gain an increasing understanding about the prophet's role. The job description gets shaped and endorsed by God and the prophet's role starts in the Old Testament and develops, with new facets, in the New Testament. Contrary to what some people think, God did not end the role of the prophets with the end of the Old Testament. As the Kingdom of Jesus Christ and His church is birthed, the Lord gives us three specific passages in the New Testament that develop the prophet's responsibility, in addition to what they have already been given in the Hebrew Scriptures. Therefore, what we see in the Old Testament becomes a standard for today, with extra requirements for the New Covenant church added into the role and job definition.

This is of the utmost importance because if we lose the foundational understanding of the role from the Old Testament, we lose all authority given to us as prophets to assist the church today to know the timings of God, the holiness of God, and the priorities of God. Nowhere in the Bible does God scrap the Old Testament principles of what a prophet should be and begin again! Instead, He enhances the role and brings extra clarity, as He requires New Covenant prophets to take on board extra tasks for the well-being and leadership of all believers. Therefore, do not ignore the Old Testament in shaping your understanding of the prophetic office.

Let's look at the three New Covenant additions to the role of prophet:

1. Prophets are foundational

> *You are no longer foreigners and strangers, but fellow citizens with God's people and also members of his household, built on the foundation of the apostles and prophets, with Christ Jesus himself as the chief cornerstone* (Ephesians 2:19-20 NIV).

Apostles and prophets become foundational to the establishing and flourishing of the household of God. We pivot around Jesus Christ, who works in conjunction with apostles and prophets to set the tone, shape, and structure by which the household thrives. This means that apostolic and prophetic ministry in the household of God is supposed to be like baking bread in your home—the aroma goes everywhere, with ease. It should not be a fight. Everyone in the house should smell revelation and it will feel natural, good, and pleasing to them. This is the heavenly atmosphere that should be in the church.

Prophets who are truly foundational do not spend their time *only* prophesying or training people to give words or bring words. Rather, they are building a prophetic culture and they are ensuring a revelatory climate is maintained. This should release and shift prophets from always feeling that they need to be bringing the "Word of the Lord" and instead into bringing the *Lord of the Word*, where everything gets shadowed in revelation. In this way, a prophetic movement underpins the House of God, and the spirit of prophecy is woven into every facet of our lives as Christians.

Consider that some prophets in Scripture have very little to say but instead create monumental shift. For example, John the Baptist, whom Jesus describes as the greatest prophet who ever lived, only gets a few lines of prophecy, but his ability to change atmospheres is great. Therefore, *prophets don't do all the prophesying!* Prophets cast a revelatory shadow that gives a value for the voice of God over everything and everyone.

The concept is reminiscent of King Saul, who comes into his right mind when shadowed by a company of prophets led by Samuel (see 1 Samuel 10:11). If we cannot let heavenly revelation shadow us and we stop the prophets from bringing their revelatory anointings, which are foundational for us all, then we will find that the church loses its right-mindedness and specifically its ability to be on time with God, for timings are the specialty of the prophetic community. (The Hebrew tribe of Issachar was the prophetic clan who knew the times and seasons and set the calendar for all the children of Israel.)

> **Foundational prophets are building a prophetic culture and ensuring a revelatory climate is maintained.**

The same principle applies to the apostolic, who must bring a saturated culture full of strategy and the ability to release and send people into their high call and into godly risk taking. My father, Pastor John Hansford, is a gifted Bible teacher and biblical literacy runs off him like rivers and waterfalls in every conversation. Lots of people who know him will testify that anytime he is in the room, and even when he is silent, he exudes a value for the authenticity and authority of the Word of God. His gift to the body of Christ is not to do all the teaching, but to give a value to the house that we need taught, and that Scripture is worth devouring for all it is worth. If you have spent any time with an evangelist, their anointing will inspire you to rededicate your life to Jesus, even if you have known Jesus and been saved by Him for many years!

So we begin to understand that the office of the prophet is a cultural role in establishing atmosphere for the House of God, as well as timings, direction, and correction. There is rarely ever a place in Scripture where a prophet turns up to pat you on the back and say, "Well done!" Their gift is the provocation that they give you to get into the right place with God and carry the right vision for what God wants to do with and through you on the earth today.

Prophecy often goes wrong in a church context when it is added as bolt-it-on to what is already happening. Desperate leaders just want to keep the weird prophetic people happy, and slightly removed from doing anything wild, dangerous, or upsetting to the established direction of travel!

But a prophetic culture is not always about taking a microphone or having a platform as a statement that the prophet or prophecy has arrived. It's not even about putting prophetic people into their own group on the sidelines. Instead, it must be a culture that comes up from the foundations. Leaders and prophetic types must work on this culture together, with relational intelligence.

2. Established Prophets Are Leaders

> *And He gave some as apostles, and some as prophets, and some as evangelists, and some as pastors and teachers, for the equipping of the saints for the work of service, to the building up of the body of Christ* (Ephesians 4:11-12 NASB95).

Prophets don't *have* a prophetic gift, they *are* a gift, chosen by God and anointed by God. They are a gift to the church and to the nations. Apostles, prophets, evangelists, pastors (shepherds), teachers—anyone in this list of five—once they are established in their fivefold office, they form the leadership structure that God puts in place and uses for the development-raising and maturity of the people of God. The prophet is part of the government and leadership of God on the earth and therefore has the responsibility to help steer and accompany the people.

3. The Prophet's Remit

In Revelation 10, John the Revelator gives us perhaps the most succinct and comprehensive understanding of what his job description involves:

> Then I was told, "You must prophesy again about many peoples, nations, languages and kings" (Revelation 10:11 NIV).

This is a prophet's remit in the New Covenant: to prophesy about peoples, nations, languages, and kings.[1] So if you've ever heard someone claim, "I'm a national prophet," or, "I'm a prophet to nations" (which are in common parlance within today's prophetic movements and on social media) it is an unnecessary thing to say. Perhaps these extra phrases simply come from the unhelpful swagger of youthful enthusiasm, but they are redundant because

> **Prophets steer the atmosphere of the church, lead the people, and prophesy to nations and kings—as God commands.**

20

when you become established as a prophet, you will have, by very definition, a remit that includes peoples, nations, languages, and kings. The office of the prophet by virtue of call gives a broad and far-reaching sphere of responsibility.

Very rarely in the body of Christ do we have a lack of authority to remove a demon, work a miracle, or receive revelation. More commonly we have a lack of mandate and permission from God to *use* that authority. We are spokespeople for God in that we speak where He says, to whom He says, to the people group He says, to the nation He says, and never according to our own preference or our own agenda.

To summarize: in addition to all that we see prophets do in the Old Testament, prophets in the New Covenant have a responsibility to 1) steer the atmosphere of the church; 2) lead the people, equipping them for works and building them up; 3) prophesy to peoples, nations, and their leaders—as God commands.

CHAPTER 2

THE OFFICE OF PROPHET VERSUS THE GIFT OF PROPHECY

AT THIS POINT, I'm sure that many of you are asking, "What about the gift of prophecy and where does it fit in with the remit of the prophet?" I wrote extensively about the gift of prophecy in my last book, *The Prophetic Warrior*. Of course, the gift of prophecy is not mentioned in the Old Testament and is only explicitly defined under the New Covenant in Paul's first letter to the Corinthians (see 1 Corinthians 12–14). While only some are called to the office of the prophet, the gift of prophecy is much more inclusive and is given that all may prophesy (see 1 Corinthians 14:31). Because the gift of prophecy is available for anyone who desires to use it, the rules for its use in Corinthians are quite defined (prophecy is for strengthening, encouragement, comfort; weigh carefully what is said). Apostle Paul pushes the concept that the gift of prophecy is about architecting hope in the lives of the receivers. In other words, there is a strong element of protecting and keeping people safe and of prioritizing personal prophetic words. Some church leaders have tended to interpret these boundaries as, "No prophesying dates, mates, or babies"—but the Bible never gives these rules!

The gift of prophecy is like a swimming pool. In the shallow end you can hear God. In the middle depths, you are becoming much more sensitive to the voice of God and the leading of His Spirit and you find yourself growing and stepping out in faith with prophetic words more often. Swimming in the deep end, you will have become a trusted prophetic voice and may even have a recognized prophetic ministry. Usually at this stage you will be able to prophesy maturely and with considerable weight and authority. A "deep end" gift of prophecy will hear God for themselves and primarily for other individuals, and for those who are not yet saved, and all of this within 1 Corinthians' parameters.

The office of the prophet cannot be found in this same swimming pool. The office of the prophet is not the deep end, it is a whole other pool! One of the greatest errors that we deal with in churches is people who are skilled within the prophetic gift then believing that they must now be or become a prophet. The gift of prophecy is given by the Holy Spirit, and all can use it, focusing on individual words. On the other hand, the office of the prophet is a vocational life call given by Jesus Christ, focusing on peoples, nations, languages, and kings.

> **The office of the prophet is in a whole other swimming pool from the prophetic gift!**

While the gift of prophecy is duty bound to comfort, edify, and strengthen one person at a time, the office of the prophet is concerned with correction and direction, the release of corporate (meaning a body of people) words, and with the shaping and structuring of the house of God—with specific remit to leaders.

A surefire way to wear out and frustrate a prophet is to ask them to only operate in the prophetic gift, demanding lots of personal ministry only and forbidding the giving of any strategic words that shape structure.

Peculiarly, God has put in Scripture a verse that limits Himself.

> *Surely the Sovereign Lord does nothing without revealing his plan to his servants the prophets* (Amos 3:7 NIV).

The Almighty Lord tells us that He will not act without first communicating with a prophet. I don't think any of us can truly grasp why God did this! It seems that He is so wired for relational interaction with His people, and that He values the office of the prophet as key to how He works on the earth, that He will withhold actions until a prophet has listened and brought into the earth realm what is on His heart.

> **God will withhold actions until a prophet has listened and brought into the earth realm what is on His heart.**

Therefore, prophets are wired to hear things first. It is why you want to spit when you are not at the center of whatever is going on! It is an anointing to hear first and to steward at the cutting edge of what God wants to do now. You feel excluded when not invited into leadership teams. Being kept out of the loop can do great damage to you relationally because you are one who is made to know ahead of others.

And, when you don't have a prophet in your local church context, you will always be playing a catch-up game with what God is doing.

A Vision of Heavenly Books

One day, when I was caught up to the heavenly realms, God put me into a new room. There were books sitting on long, high tables, as far as the eye could see. I knew these were the books of the story of the earth. Some were history books; others were books of things yet to happen; one had a spotlight on it and it was for what God wanted to see happen in the earth right now. Angels came into this room and went to the books of the earth's history and started to weep as they opened them. They ripped out many pages with lists of people's names on them and removed these pages to a separate archive room. Bewildered, I asked God what was happening. He told me that what the angels were removing were things that God wanted to see happen but that there was no prophet on the earth who was attentively listening, and so it could not come to pass. The angels were upset that many had not come to know Jesus because prophets had not heard God's desire to bring revival during their lifetimes.

Prayer

Jesus, we cry out to You in repentance for not being attentive to what was coming out of Your mouth and instead filling the air with what was coming out of our own mouths.

Would You have mercy on us for our demanding ways, when we wanted You to bless what we were doing, and we forgot to ask what You were doing. We are sorry that we forgot to ask what excited You and what plans You had for the earth during our lifetime!

Father God, would You take us by the hand and lead us in a lifestyle of attentively listening, so that we might become the voice of what You want to accomplish in the earth.

In Jesus' name, amen.

CHAPTER 3

PROPHETS AND THE FIVEFOLD MINISTRY

JESUS IS AN apostle, prophet, shepherd, teacher, and evangelist. His life and ministry was the most perfect example of all the five offices that we read in Ephesians chapter 4. When Jesus left the earth realm and ascended into glory, He divided His anointings into these five specializations or five church leadership functions. Ephesians 4:8 (NIV) tells us that, "When he ascended on high, he took many captives and gave gifts to his people."

Let's consider these verses again:

> *And He gave some as apostles, and some as prophets, and some as evangelists, and some as pastors and teachers, for the equipping of the saints for the work of service, to the building up of the body of Christ* (Ephesians 4:11-12 NASB95).

Apostle, prophet, shepherd, teacher, and evangelist are the gifts (also referred to by some as the "fivefold graces" or "fivefold offices") that Jesus gave to the church, post-ascension, to reflect who He had been on the earth.

In giving us different specializations that together represent the fullness of Jesus Christ, we are being pushed into teamwork and an acknowledgment that we need each other to fully represent Him. To be Jesus to the world, all five must been seen and active. All five must be given space to flourish and, importantly, given opportunities to sharpen each other. This is not a mere Pentecostal doctrine or a new-fangled idea. It is a Jesus doctrine. It's the way Jesus gave us to structure His church and to best represent who He is, so that we would be raised to unity and maturity. If one of these attributes of Jesus is missing from your decision-making tables, you will not represent Jesus comprehensively and you will not be able to make decisions that bring all that He is to your area.

If all you have are shepherds and teachers, but you have no evangelists, you will nurture the sheep and systematically train the sheep, but you will never have growth, and you will bore your people with repetition and coziness.

If you are apostolically and prophetically wired but you have no shepherds, people will love the strategy, risk taking, and timings of God, but they will feel unnurtured. You will have a large, welcoming front door to your church because you will sound amazing. But you will also have an equally large back door through which the people will want to exit very fast when they realize that no one looks after them! This combination produces the most transient congregations.

I love the kind of conversation that having all five offices seated together brings. Apostles and prophets can often hog the airspace, talking over-excitedly with *drama!* and *risk!* while the shepherd quietly chimes in that if we do things in a purely apostolic and prophetic way not a single sheep will come with us and be *emotionally well.* The evangelist will drive numbers because they want to get as many saved as possible—they always think a stadium event is the ultimate strategic goal! (At this the shepherd will begin to gently weep in the corner, desiring small groups so that nurture can be felt.) The teacher just wants to train everybody because they know that if the people could just hear the Word of God with robust biblical unpacking, then everybody's character issues will get fixed.

Each of the fivefold feels deeply that if you just did it *their* way it would bring the most transformation! The reality is that all five must learn submission to each other's strengths and specializations and to discern when each one needs to shine to keep us all looking like Jesus. They need to know which combination is needed at each moment in church life.

By now we should be absolutely killing any lie or misconception that there are only one or two apostles and prophets in a nation. This nonsense is usually touted by small-minded people who are playing a power game, led by an empire spirit that likes to secure control. The truth is that we need an explosion of expertise and maturity across all fivefold functions.

Old Testament Israel was a relatively small nation and yet it had a minimum of six highly functioning prophetic schools or companies, where prophets lived together and developed their specialization for the well-being of the nation. These include Gibeah and Ramah, where Samuel had schools of prophets. Both the company of prophets in Bethel and Jericho (with together at least 50 prophets) are part of the story of Elijah being taken up to Heaven in the second chapter of 2 Kings. We find another company by the Jordan, expanding the place where they live, and Gilgal has one hundred prophets in one place! The fact that some of them are spoken about as "schools of the prophets" indicates flourishing growth, replication, and ongoing training. All of this indicates a quantity of prophets and quality developmental programs, even for one relatively small land area. We will look at companies and "nests" of prophets again in later chapters.

Though our focus together in this book is to become the voice of God (in other words, becoming a prophet), we do need to gain a robust understanding of what each of the fivefold attributes of Jesus does, so that we have a good grasp of their strengths and weaknesses, and how we each might best work together to build up the church.

SHEPHERDS

You might be surprised to know that, despite its ubiquitous use for leaders in the church today, the word *pastor* is not found anywhere in modern English translations of the Bible. Of course, the word shepherd is, and it was Calvin's translation of Ephesians 4:11 back in the 16th century that gave us this unique idea of translating shepherd as pastor—just for this one verse and nowhere else.[1] Shepherd is the more accurate and consistent translation.

A shepherd's anointing is laden with kindness. They are carers, and they bring the social glue to a community. You will feel nurtured, guarded, and protected with them. They bring a contagious unity and maintain communal health with a loving vibe. They are the "soul healers" of the body of Christ. They affirm what is human within a structure. They are wired for empathy, and their decision making is based on inclusiveness and stability with a communal impulse. This means that they move slowly, so that no one is left out—because they believe in a lifelong spiritual development and protracted encouragement. More than any other anointing they adore unity and cohesion. They might on occasion bore you—but you'll always feel safe!

When the entire church community is dominated by shepherd leaders you will have a strong and relentless focus on unity movements, leaving little time to engage with some key Bible thoughts such as Ecclesiastes 3:5, which teaches that you must know the difference between the times to embrace and the time to refrain. Or the verses in Matthew 10 that necessitate that there will be disunity among family members when the remnant separates from the nominal church. The next few years of the 21st century are really going to stretch the shepherds as we enter the age of the church split,[2] where Jesus prophesied of the birthing of a remnant who love not their own life, and who have bought the costly oil of intimacy. They will separate from those who adhere to Jesus Christ in name only.

> **A shepherd's decision making is based on inclusiveness and stability with a communal impulse.**

Shepherds can too easily become a "doormat," engulfed in false responsibility and a desire to always say "yes" to people. They usually get maxed out at leading around 120-150 church members because they need to know the names and stories of every single one of "their people." The worst thing you can do to a shepherd is to use words that make them feel pressurized to grow their church. In today's culture, which is always pushing for church growth, they can feel like failures—they are very happy in small to medium-sized rooms.

I was raised by a shepherd-teacher and have complete admiration for the necessary atmosphere of nourishment they provide.

EVANGELISTS

Evangelists are the recruiters to the cause, and they gather with a contagious storytelling. They love good news! They are people orientated, of course, but I'm sorry to say that they are only temporarily interested in you because they continually need a steady flow of strangers to bring to Jesus! Evangelists are naturally infectious, and they enlist people, sell their products, and promote the significance of the company they work for. Evangelists are social connectors who link up the world.

Above every other fivefold office, the evangelists are motivated by large rooms, and the bigger the numbers, the more strategic it feels to them. They are often unimpressed with inner healing and anything that requires extended ministry processes, because "Surely Jesus did it all at the cross and you instantly get transformed when you meet Him!" So don't expect evangelists to love process or to sit well in a small room. They love to be relevant, and they have a high value for demonstrations of the power of God which lead people to Jesus; therefore, expect power miracles around them wherever they go.

> **Evangelists love good news and have a high value for demonstrations of the power of God.**

A Prophetic Caution to Evangelists

Allow me to take a moment to issue a caution to the evangelistically minded. I am concerned that we are in great danger of "car crashing" the development of the church by preaching a modern gospel of salvation versus the gospel of the Kingdom, which is what Jesus preached.

In the limited gospel message of salvation, the focus is merely on Jesus becoming your personal Savior. If this is all a new believer is taught to understand, we will completely contain Jesus to the point where He becomes a "sugar daddy in the sky" who we think is there to bend to meet our personal needs. This teaching lacks any sense of His magisterial kingship! If Jesus is only expressed as a personal Savior, then you overlook (and perhaps even deny) that He is the King of an advancing Kingdom. But when you come to Christ through the gospel of the Kingdom, your start point is to bow low and confess that Jesus Christ is your Lord—you submit to the King who is already on the throne, and you enter His Kingdom with the understanding that you have a proactive part to play in the development and advancing of His reign. When new converts understand that we both enter a relationship with Jesus Christ as much as we enter membership of a Kingdom at salvation, their entire approach to living the Christian life changes.

Salvation is a staged process where we repent of our sins; believe in the Lord Jesus Christ as Savior *and* as Lord; are baptized in water; receive the Holy Spirit—that is what it means to be born again. The New Testament never discusses the concept of Jesus as a *personal* savior. Yes, of course we need to be saved but we come to Him as both Savior *and* Lord to be saved. Why does this matter? Because, if we adhere to the incorrect, modern, evangelical cliché, then we do away with ideas of submission and participation. Having only met Jesus as Savior means you can *receive* from Him but not *yield* to Him. But when we correctly teach the gospel of the Kingdom, then we will approach Jesus with a greater, rightful reverence and fear, with complete submission, acknowledging His role as King of Kings and Lord of Lords!

We have much work to do to unseat this incorrect concept of the gospel of salvation, which has led generations into selective surrender and partial yielding because their initial meeting of Jesus was wrongly framed. This re-framing of how we belong to God and one another enables us to submit to one another and to put our hands collectively to what enables the thriving of the Kingdom. Remember, in the Lord's prayer we do not pray, "Your salvation come," we pray, "Your Kingdom come!"

TEACHERS

Like the shepherds, teachers are in it for the long haul. They thrive in bringing and curating spaces for lifelong learning, and they ground the body of Christ, creating an atmosphere for contagious learning. They are the effective trainers, the inspirers of investigation of the Bible, the philosophers, and the thinkers who bring wisdom and understanding. They love books. Teachers stay within the "go slow" gears of a car, because they live by the rule that for as long as you live you will be sharpened by teaching, bit by bit, sermon by sermon. If Sunday services are not sequentially developing people, they get nervous. Teachers are rattled by organic and spontaneous decision-making! But they are dependable and reliable truth-unpackers,

> Teachers are rattled by organic and spontaneous decision-making! But they are dependable and reliable truth-unpackers.

believing that if they can get enough detailed theology into you, you will make better decisions in your life.

Teachers have an uphill struggle ahead of them in the coming years because we live in a "post-truth culture." This means that the concept of "absolute truth" has been almost completely erased and our society increasingly believes that you can choose your own truth. This has brought an intimidation to the body of Christ that has caused her to mute herself out of the fear of bringing offense to those whose own truth doesn't marry up with absolute, biblical truth. Jesus declared that absolute truth sets us free and that He is the way, the truth, and the life, and so it means we have a greater responsibility than we have currently taken on board to speak, and teach, absolute truth. We stopped saying to those in sexual perversion that they could be healed and that Jesus had a better way for them, and so in our silence we endorsed their lifestyle.

Perhaps my greatest prayer for my own children is taken from Psalm 45, where we are told to *love* righteousness and *hate* wickedness. I pray that they would have such a passion for righteous truth that it would provoke, as Scripture says, an emotional response in them—that their heart would be in love with right behavior and truth, and that the opposite would also be true— that they would be motivated to despise wickedness and things that would turn their heads away from Jesus.

Our emotional response to righteousness and wickedness is supposed to be quite extreme! We thought, wrongly, that love looked like toleration. But God is love, not "love is God"! We must begin with *who God is* as a standard for how we love. In other words, we begin with God to define what love is. And we begin with God to define what truth is.

A Prophetic Prayer Over Teachers

Teachers, I release over you, in Jesus' name, a liberation of your voice to become one who will fight intimidation and teach and unpack Scripture in the fear of God, resetting His standards in your congregations and beyond.

APOSTLES

Apostles are the strategists, the visionaries, and the entrepreneurs. They govern with contagious empowerment. They are the sent ones, sent as gifts to help us structure, shape, strategize, and set order. Apostles put a framework in place for us all to thrive. They are sent to pioneer the new; they start movements and innovative business ventures. They are sent by God to turn around and recalibrate the structures when they fail us. They become absolutely pivotal in changing seasons or epochs, which is why we really need to bless them now, for we have much need of them.

> Apostles are pivotal in changing seasons, which is why we really need to bless them now, for we have much need of them.

Most apostles will have a people or a geography that they are sent to mobilize for movement and broad impact. Not only are they sent, but they also *send* people, meaning that they have an outward-looking instinct and are often bored in micromanagement. Apostles like the big picture and the macro-overviews. If you catch them or contain them in the micromanagement of the day to day, you will ultimately wear them out. They have a natural capacity for adventure and risk and are usually fast paced. Apostles are custodians of the core DNA of the church, and they know what church should be—a place of power and impact. Apostles are happiest in a small, strategic group.

A Prophecy to Apostles

I have seen in the spirit realm a military-surge anointing coming to a selected group of apostles. It is like an energy landing on their core that will enable them to push the body of Christ to where it needs to be. This anointing will liberate them from the wearing of Saul's armor. In other words, this is freedom from wearing clothes that fitted a previous generation but are now like old wineskins. This will include ceasing to labor under what was another man's framework. They will be purified apostles who tear off the old mantles. For the Lord would say to you, "Do not try to see which parts of the old ways you can take through the door of today. The good that was in the old must be torn off. Leave behind what was good yesterday, and what was even a purposeful identity. Stop tying the old methods to the new anointing."

God says to the apostles that a new anointing will come with cost, and you will need to grow into an example of casting off what used to fit you well, so that you will be able to carry the power and the blessing of this fresh anointing in leadership.

This anointing will enable apostles to throw off the need to control. Instead, they will liberate, in love, many into their high call. It is a Davidic apostolicity where they are after God's heart rather than the adulation of man. It is the birth of the warrior apostles, who push back darkness and engage in spiritual warfare to the same degree that they engage in strategizing and structuring.

For the Lord would say to the apostolic leaders, "I need you to be in the Spirit as much as you are in the practical strategy."

Many church members bear the pain of over-religious and controlling leaders. However, we must be careful as followers to make sure that we are not easily offended and lacking open, receptive spirits to the necessary sharpening that leadership is supposed to bring. A leader-follower relationship is, after all, two-way. At the same time, God is not asking us to pay our offerings, tithes, and sacrifices into leaders and places who no longer have God's favor, because they treated the sheep as an audience to be controlled rather than as an army to be equipped, mobilized, sent, and trusted.

This is a time when God is bringing a long, slow humiliation to leaders in the public arena (politicians and celebrities). The Lord is allowing their lack of integrity to be fully seen, so that men no longer trust in worldly systems. Watch for the slow discrediting of many in high public office, in order that God can have a harvest of souls who are fed up with the style of leadership that they see in the world and who are provoked by their disappointment to seek King Jesus—because they want a Man they can follow!

The Lord says that church leadership has not kept pace or matured into the required new level and that there will even be a closing of Bible colleges and seminaries who do not know how to train emerging leaders in how to lead in a season of war. But God now calls the apostolic "war leadership schools" open in the spirit realm for you to pull down and make reality. A new grace is given to those who will establish new leadership and church training programs, who are steeped in Holy Spirit thinking rather than man-made strategy.

There is a great healing move of God that will land on the unhealed hearts and flesh of senior leadership, where God will assist you to get rid of your wounds that came from when you carried a great weight of loss and pain and yet stayed the course amid hardship. Jesus Christ is beside, and within, His leaders.

PROPHETS

Prophets are the guides who come alongside the people of God to steer and influence them in the building of the Kingdom of God on the earth. In Ezra's day, the prophets Haggai and Zechariah supported the rebuilding of the temple alongside Ezra the teacher, Zerubbabel the apostle, Nehemiah the apostle, and Joshua and his team of shepherds.

> *Then Zerubbabel son of Shealtiel and Joshua son of Jozadak set to work to rebuild the house of God in Jerusalem. And the prophets of God were with them, supporting them* (Ezra 5:2 NIV).

This was a prototype of fivefold ministry work, working together almost five centuries before the birth of the church. It was a high-powered team of leaders, bringing their key anointings and specializations, pulling together for the success of the house of God. It is a prime example of strength in diversity that we must not overlook just because it is in the Old Testament.

Prophets have contagious insight and look deeply to reveal the motivations of the heart. They are visionaries who see the future and call it into being. They are mantled by the Lord to maintain faithfulness to Him in the lives of His people. Prophets are profoundly aware of God's heart and are often found working in issues of justice, law, and environmental responsibilities.

They are happy in high-risk and fast-paced decision situations, and always have a sense of urgency and immediacy about them. To the prophet, change needs to happen, "Now!"

A Word to Prophets Today

At the moment of time that we are in, there is a deep purifying happening to the prophets. We are in the "second wave" of the prophetic movement, moving past the error of the political fascinations of some previous prophets, who wrongly believed that what happened in the sphere of politics defined a nation. The last three years revealed that the prophets did not know how to call people into repentance. We were only bold in words that aligned with the national culture and political trajectory.

But we are the "post-COVID-pandemic prophetic movement." We are the "wartime prophetic movement"—warring for truth and for life!

We clearly have a leadership crisis in the nations (this is not just in the church). Inaction, fear, and self-protection is found in almost all the leaders in public life across society. Why is this? It is because the prophets did not have fresh revelation! When a leader hears the word of the Lord, it gives them courage to act rightly. If you do not have a brave prophet, you cannot have a courageous leader. Wherever you see poor leadership, look at the absence of visionary revelation around them.

> **If you do not have a brave prophet, you cannot have a courageous leader.**

The Lord says to the prophets, "Prophets, you have robbed leaders right across the board of courage, because you were in franchise-based models that were echoes, and you were in-fighting rather than behaving Kingdom-mindedly. You have robbed others of hope—and robbed Me in the process—of many souls because of what and how you spoke, but mainly because you did not speak for Me as you should."

The prophets didn't know who they were. God now says to them, "Will you let Me redefine you and put you through a winnowing fire? I am going to ask you to do things that are militant and uncomfortable. I am going to give you a new understanding of holiness and I will provoke you to purpose—so that you can provoke others into their purpose."

In the absence of the true authority of King Jesus coursing through our veins, other authority has taken over. But prophets, this is to be the day when your revelation will collide with the Kingdom of God and with the authority of God!

The Lord says that it is time to end ego-boosting prophetic words that pander to insecurities, for now we must prophesy to release strength in the

> **Prophets are mantled by God to maintain faithfulness to Him in the lives of His people.**

earth, cultivate the hearts of men and women, bring forth God's timings, and release courage.

- Without the prophets, the church chooses political correctness.

- Without the prophets, the church chooses false safety.

- Without the prophets, the church chooses to protect and defend rather than advance and possess.

- Without the prophets, the church prefers its history to its future.

- Without the prophets, people idolize men rather than God—they invest in man-made structures.

- Without the prophets, there is no ability for courageous leaders to arise for they cannot see the future alone.

A Prayer for Prophets

Prophets, I pray for you right now in Jesus' name, to not be shattered internally but to be able to bear the weight of the fullness of your call. I loose to you an ability to stand in the pressure and the winnowing fire of God that will come to you in this season, so that you might enter another level of glory. I release an ability for you to stand and for you to be consumed by glory fire of God. I liberate you into a partnership with undefiled revelation, that you might receive the heart and the motivations of God—and God alone. Amen.

CHAPTER 4

Prophets and the Church

OVERALL, THE CHURCH has functioned with a dominant pastoral and teaching leadership paradigm for hundreds of years. This has resulted in many prophets speaking with a pastoral mindset, not realizing that they had a prophetic mindset to step into. After all, the only places you could serve in the church in bygone days were through pastoring and teaching—or children's or women's ministry.

In light of this, prophets wrongly put on a pastoral voice that wasn't theirs, with a shepherding sound and mindset, just to be accepted. We forgot what it was to have a prophet's voice, a prophet's sound, and a prophet's anointing. When a prophet's thought process and language did happen to sneak out, it was often shut down, and so we retreated back into the pastoral paradigm. However, the prophetic is going to go through a massive shift, and prophets *will* start to think and speak like prophets!

Love looks different in each of the fivefold offices. Shepherding love is *safe,* as is teaching love. Therefore, a prophet wearing the clothes of a shepherd will look at someone and seek to give them words of sweet nurture, adulation, a settling in their current trajectory, reinforcement of who they are, and confirmation of their call. Usually, it feels a bit like an ego boost and pulls on confirming words like *love, blessing, promotion, advancing, speed*, and *breakthrough*.

However, absolutely nowhere in Scripture do we see that prophecy is only ever to be confirmation alone. In fact, it is quite the opposite! Prophecy is often *new* information brought to challenge you and to redirect you. It releases hitherto unheard battle strategies and peculiar activations that will lead you into wellness (think of Naaman washing seven times in the river Jordan to be healed of leprosy in 2 Kings 5). Never in the Bible do we read of a prophet saying to someone, "Well done, you've got nothing to change—you just carry on exactly as you are, you are currently a roaring success in every way, and God is going to promote you right now!"

On the other hand, apostolic and prophetic love is risky. It does not ask, "How *nurtured* can I make you feel?" Rather it thinks, "How free can I get you?" It is a liberating love that grabs the horizon line of your life and lets you see it, because you will aim at what you can see. Prophets take risks with words on your behalf to bring you into processes of purification and new understandings of who God says you are. Their words expose why and where things have gone wrong and give redemptive action plans.

> Prophetic love is a risky, liberating love that grabs the horizon line of your life and lets you see it so that you can aim for it.

THE LORD'S REBUKE TO PROPHETS

> *Prophets, you have dumbed yourselves down to be accepted. You spoke like shepherds, not prophets. Worse still, at times you spoke like teachers, where recipients of the word felt patronized and belittled by your dressing up your teaching opinion as a prophetic word.*

Each of the fivefold offices, in a well-functioning church, should have their specific distinctives celebrated, not feared.

PROPHETS IN TRADITIONAL CHURCH STRUCTURES

Let's take an honest look at the church as she is today. The traditional church structures predominantly tend to sit as a limiting cap on the full flourishing of everybody within the fivefold offices. We are not as healthily wired as we should be for the celebration of those who exceed our own capabilities or have strengths in areas that we don't. Perhaps we are more easily threatened by the promotion of others than we would like to acknowledge? Tragically, people who are pushing successfully into the call of God on their lives have often not had space to flourish. Too frequently they find themselves outside what the church can cope with. They accidently become enemies of the church and leave, rather than become fundamental to the running of the church.

> We are not as healthily wired as we should be for the celebration of those who exceed our own capabilities or have strengths in areas that we don't.

Typically, it is the apostles and prophets who leave because by calling they are the "get up and go" temperaments, whereas the shepherds, teachers, and evangelists are the "stay and grow" people.

In addition, women have traditionally been overlooked by church culture. Therefore, anointed, gifted women have, for many generations, had to leave the church to thrive—or else they have had to completely silence themselves. I remember receiving much encouragement many decades ago while working in pharmaceuticals when a lady prophesied saying that the Lord would bless me outlandishly in the secular environment and would keep me there until the church could find a place of honor for me. I felt relieved that God had a plan that enabled enjoyment of the place that I found myself in, with a patient understanding of the verse, "*A person's gift makes room for him and brings him before great people*" (Proverbs 18:16 NASB).

My late mother, who was from a previous generation, was a prophet (though she didn't know this for the first sixty years of her life) and was extremely gifted. I watched as she had to wrestle for decades with her place in church life, even as a pastor's wife. She labored with much misunderstanding around about her, and with the church's instinctive desire to contain all that was in her, which was brilliant, shining, and gloriously strong.

She was not rebellious; she was just capable. As I share her story, can we collectively acknowledge that this struggle is real and painful? I remember her tears in my adult years after I had begun full-time ministry—tears of joy for me, and tears of what felt like wasted years to her. A conversation is etched in my mind of her saying that she felt like she had lost parts of her and had had to hide them to stay within the walls of the church. We have to be honest enough to acknowledge that, while God secured her legacy in the earth and turned things around for good, she also went to heaven at her death with portions of unfulfillment in her heart and some degree of disappointment about what might have been had the church been more open to diverse anointings.

I deliberately share my family story with you because it is authentic and real, and I know that it is probably where some of you are right now. Let's pray:

> *In Jesus' name, I bless you to heal for all the pain you received, knowingly and unknowingly, at the hands of the church. I speak healing for all the times that you have been overlooked, demeaned, or belittled. I release life from the throne of God fully back into your being to restore every place of bruising that came from being misunderstood. May the Holy Spirit now bring to remembrance the gifts of God that are within you, and may you be strengthened to stand again to play your full part in the Kingdom of God. In Jesus' name, I decree effectual and fruitful doors to be open to you!*

LEADING A FLOURISHING FIVEFOLD MINISTRY

"Isn't it amazing that we are all made in God's image and yet there is so much diversity among His people?"

—DESMOND TUTU,
late Archbishop of South Africa

The desire to be special and significant is cut deep into our souls. We are not made clones but are called to soar in the diverse anointings we have been given. The spiritual anointings and riches within you will be used by God and will open up doors for you.

A controlled culture that is homogenous will no longer assist us in becoming the victorious church. Each anointing, each aspect of the fivefold, flies high in an atmosphere of liberty and freedom. However, the good news is that it *is* perfectly possible to curate atmospheres and entire cultures where no one is disposable, and yet at the same time, where we submit one to another, and where leadership still sets the tone and is ultimately responsible. As a leader of a fivefold team, all of this can be slightly terrifying because of the extreme diversity, differing approaches, and competing priorities of each of these varied anointings. Add into these other relational dynamics such as different personality types and people's perceived understanding (or misunderstanding) of their own level of maturity. Well, truly we can say that in this atmosphere of freedom there will never be no oxen in the stall, but you will always be cleaning up a mess![1]

For a leader, having the fivefold all flourishing within your house will press every button you have about being in control. You will be in charge—and spiritually the buck will stop with you—but the DNA and culture that you are a custodian of is the DNA of Heaven and not solely your own. What and who you will lead will be more diverse than you, and more gifted than you in many areas. This will necessitate you being very healed to lead a fivefold ministry well. God likes it that way. Most of us will live with some sort of subtle triggering of our unhealed parts all the time. We must notice our triggers—who annoys us and why, what makes us angry, what triggers us to dominate? Then we must decide not to call people *out* and shame them, but instead to call them *up* and to call them *into* something of greater fruit while we keep our hearts in check and continually live a whole, healed lifestyle.

If you are not a leader, you must invest quality time in relationships with your leaders and leadership team so that you are relationally safe enough to be trusted with using a provoking call like that of the prophet. Being relationally safe equals being trusted to prophesy.

God's formula in His structuring of church governance is unity through diversity. Our fear of diversity in anointings has become a real issue in church culture. But a fear-free culture gives joy to its people because it celebrates highly successful, diversified strengths.

It is only when all five anointings have a place at the decision-making table that truly good decisions that reflect Jesus can be made (remember that earlier we looked at how Jesus is the perfect example of each of the fivefold offices). You will make bad leadership decisions if you only listen to one aspect of the nature of Jesus Christ. You will irritate and cause pain to those in your care if you exclude an aspect of the fivefold ministry just because you couldn't get biblical and get comfortable with their specialization. And, because we make better decisions when every one of the fivefold roles is represented in the room, this means that you will need

> We make decisions more like Jesus when every one of the fivefold roles is represented. You will need a prophet on your leadership team.

prophets on your leadership team! *Together* you will develop balance about your core activities. This is not a trivial matter. The whole maturity of the body depends on this: it is through the successful functioning of the fivefold that maturity comes.

If you don't have each of these voices represented *in leadership*, then you will be unable to represent Jesus Christ fully. Cozy leadership that is only with those who "get you" loses the vital need of sharpening of each other.

If one of the fivefold anointing is outside of leadership, then you will open up *all* the people you lead to problems. If the people you lead cannot see their core value (such as prophecy) represented within a leadership dynamic, they will either attempt prophetic hijacking of the platform (trying to get the essence of what they carry represented with unhelpful words, forced or grabbed at any opportunity they spot when they can release them), or else you will be contending with an "Absalom Spirit."

Absalom was King David's son (see 1 Samuel 13 onward) who sat outside the city gates, undermining David's leadership and eventually plotting against him to take his crown. He schemed for years, seeking his father's utter ruin. How did he get to that ugly place? Initially, Absalom partnered with great offense at King David's perceived inaction over the rape of Absalom's sister Tamar. His offense became judgment, and the judgment became bitterness—which is emotionally cancerous.

This Absalom Spirit will spread around a congregation and is marked by the dishonor and discrediting of leadership. It will also seek its own platform at the expense of everyone else. Of course, we can easily and accidentally offend each other—it's part of the rough and tumble of almost all relationships—but if we cannot (or will not) keep "short accounts" internally, in which our offense is speedily overturned, allowing love to cover a multitude of sins (see 1 Peter 4:8), it will soon develop into judgment and bitterness.

After many years of church leadership, I have come to the conclusion that when relationships progress beyond offense and decline into judgment and bitterness, there is rarely any ability to work together left. At this point it is better that all geographical proximity and shared activity come to an end. Therefore:

- Leaders: do not create Absaloms, who will be a thorn in your flesh and a destroyer of your reputation and leadership authority, just because you did not create space for the fivefold to flourish under your leadership.
- Church members: if you have become an Absalom and your frustration is now a judgment against leadership, you must leave that church quietly and lovingly, because you have set your heart against leadership. You must move on for everybody's well-being.

As we push into the development of fivefold ministry in our church settings, it can take a congregation quite a while to get comfortable with the rhythm of having a fivefold leadership team. It takes a covenantal bond within the leadership to hold together. It is worth discussing this bond as a team, so that everyone understands the depths of connection required. This kind of biblical leadership is a lifestyle, not a hobby.

Shepherding and teaching have been so embedded as church core values, missing that the biblical foundation is actually on the apostles and prophets, that it means there is a degree of course correction needed in the default "tone" of the church. We have had nurture—but no long-term planning for transformation of cities and nations. Our values have been for what we did *in* the church and never outside it. We are inward-looking and risk averse.

> The new reformation of the church needs strong, gifted, apostolic and prophetic leaders, who are brave enough to make some extreme decisions that will look like foolishness in the eyes of man.

The recent years have taken us through shaking and dismantling, and now we stand at the door of the reformation of the church once again. This will absolutely necessitate strong, gifted, apostolic and prophetic leaders who are brave—brave enough to make some extreme decisions that will look like foolishness in the eyes of man but will be wisdom before God. Shepherds, teachers, and evangelists will need to add to the flock and nurture the flock in the changing dynamic, but they must not be resistant of the need for change. Change is the new normal!

CHAPTER 5

PROPHETS AND
BIBLICAL LEADERSHIP

EMERGING VERSUS ESTABLISHED PROPHETS

By now many of you reading this book might be beginning to think that you have a call to be a prophet. If so, you're probably starting to ask questions like, "How do I even commence the journey toward becoming an established, recognized prophet?" For a number of years, I have trained hundreds of new prophets through a two-year (and beyond) Raising Prophets mentoring program in Scotland. In its early years we called this course, and everyone who signed up to it, emerging prophets,[1] which to me is a perfect phrase to describe the beginnings of the journey into the call of the prophet. What's the difference between an "emerging" prophet and an "established" prophet? Let's go back to our New Testament key verses:

> *So Christ himself gave the apostles, the prophets, the evangelists, the pastors and teachers, to equip his people for works of service, so that the body of Christ may be built up until we all reach unity in the faith*

and in the knowledge of the Son of God and become mature, attaining to the whole measure of the fullness of Christ.

Then we will no longer be infants, tossed back and forth by the waves, and blown here and there by every wind of teaching and by the cunning and craftiness of people in their deceitful scheming. Instead, speaking the truth in love, we will grow to become in every respect the mature body of him who is the head, that is, Christ. From him the whole body, joined and held together by every supporting ligament, grows and builds itself up in love, as each part does its work (Ephesians 4:11-16 NIV).

The whole passage above pivots on the word *equip*. The five-fold are primarily given to *equip His people*. For sure, they are leaders—but they lead by *equipping*. This is the New Covenant foundational instruction for leadership and is a completely different concept from being led to fit the behavior, the function, and the activity of church services. The equipping has an aim of unity and maturity; the measurement of the maturity is knowing Jesus more and being filled with Christ.

ESTABLISHED PROPHETS ARE LEADERS WHO EQUIP

Equipping leadership proactively raises others up. It teaches and trains, bringing people to a condition of fitness, perfecting them into a prepared and ready state. Followers are properly adjusted, in good working order, brought to an exact fit so that they can effectively function in their call in the Kingdom. This concept of equipping carries such a value of liberation and release, it is qualifying people for greater works by investment in them. This is the heart of an established prophet, or indeed any other office in its mature form. The job of leaders in the fivefold is to bring shape, so that you work perfectly!

You are only an established prophet when we can measure your equipping capabilities in the lives of others. Equipping means replication, multiplication, and the ability to teach the Bible. Therefore, to assess how established and mature a prophet is requires measuring how many they have led into revelatory maturity themselves—along with the weighable quality of the words they have received from God.

> The heart of any fivefold office is to equip people for greater works by investing in them.

To say, "I prophesy, therefore I should be a prophet" is just not a biblical thought. If you can prophesy within a relationally flourishing place but you are not yet preparing and raising a group to maturity, you are *emerging*. It is only in the building and equipping of others that you gain the authority from God to lead and to be classed as a functioning member of the fivefold.

Only some prophets mature to the level of equipping others. There are many who have called themselves prophets and

> It is only in the building and equipping of others that you gain the authority from God to lead and to be classed as a functioning member of the fivefold.

travel the world or post on social media using that title, but they are only in the emerging form (and therefore lacking significant authority) because Ephesians 4 adds to their job responsibility the requirement and ability to equip and to replicate. This is why we see, read, and hear some prophets prophesy but we see little change. Their words lack transformative power because they lack authority.

A true prophet is one who has proven maturity to equip others *and* has seen this ability to equip become their major tenet of service to the body of Christ. Perhaps until they have the maturity and experience to begin equipping others, we need to limit ourselves to saying that someone is "operating with an apostolic grace" or a "prophetic grace" rather than saying they are an "apostle" or "prophet." Similarly, a mature evangelist doesn't do all the work of reaching the lost; rather, they *equip* the saints to reach the lost. A true fivefold teacher *equips* the saints in knowledge, but also helps them to teach others (replication). A myriad of recent surveys of church leaders have revealed that anywhere between 42 percent and 90 percent of pastors report that they are depressed or burnt out. Why? Because they are doing all the shepherding rather than equipping others to shepherd.

BIBLICAL LEADERSHIP

Paul, writing to the Corinthians, is clear that, under the dancing hand of the Holy Spirit, spiritual gifts are given to all believers.

> *There are different kinds of gifts, but the same Spirit distributes them. There are different kinds of service, but the same Lord. There are different kinds of working, but in all of them and in everyone it is the same God at work.*

Now to each one the manifestation of the Spirit is given for the common good. To one there is given through the Spirit a message of wisdom, to another a message of knowledge by means of the same Spirit, to another faith by the same Spirit, to another gifts of healing by that one Spirit, to another miraculous powers, to another prophecy, to another distinguishing between spirits, to another speaking in different kinds of tongues, and to still another the interpretation of tongues. All these are the work of one and the same Spirit, and he distributes them to each one, just as he determines (1 Corinthians 12:4-11 NIV).

Every believer is gifted by God to some degree with prophecy, healing, faith, tongues, interpretation of tongues, discerning of spirits, words of wisdom, words of knowledge, or miraculous powers—the nine gifts of the spirit. (Whether they choose to use them or not is a different conversation!) We believe in the indwelling Spirit of God, indwelling all who profess faith; therefore, *all* have spiritual capabilities and powers in the name of Jesus. This is the "believer level" of ministry.

Specialization comes as the next step, in which we enter the "ministry level" of our call and we grow specific skills and a depth of partnership with the Spirit of God in one area. Following on from this, there is a step up to the "leadership level" of call, denoting a defined, fixed vocation. We see that all believers are anointed, some develop ministry specialization, and an even smaller group are chosen as leaders.

- Believer Level—all have spiritual gifts
- Ministry Level—growing in specific gifts

- Leadership Level—a call, or a vocation, to a gift or office.

The Bible is not a detailed encyclopedia, science paper, or devotional grab bag to make you feel good. It is God's story—the Father's story of how He wins back His wayward children. In it, He gives us a framework for biblical leadership and the required virtues of leaders in public life, but He does not give us the minutiae of details for setting up leadership structures. Instead, we must embark on a joyful dig into Scripture. After all, *"It is the glory of God to conceal a matter; to search out a matter is the glory of kings"* (Proverbs 25:2 NIV).

Let's look at the chronological written order of Paul's letters to the churches. This timed order of when God released truth through Paul to the church will help us build a picture of how we might order and structure our church leadership. If God released these truths in a specific order, it seems appropriate that we might accordingly build from that order.

A good estimate for the dating of Paul's letters is:[2]

1. Galatians (Antioch, A.D. 48?)

2. 1 and 2 Thessalonians (Corinth, A.D. 50)

3. 1 Corinthians (Ephesus, A.D. 55)

4. Philippians 3:2–4:9 (Ephesus, A.D. 55?)

5. 2 Corinthians (Macedonia, A.D. 56)

6. Romans (Corinth, A.D. 57)

7. Philippians 1:1–3:1 and 4:10–23 (Rome, A.D. 60/61)

8. Colossians, Philemon, and Ephesians (Rome, A.D. 60/61?)

9. 1 Timothy (Macedonia, after A.D. 62?)

10. 2 Timothy (Rome, A.D. 65?)

11. Titus (Rome, A.D. 65-67?)[3]

Most of our guidance on church leadership comes from three of these letters, those to the Ephesians, Titus, and Timothy. As we can see from the list above, of these, Ephesians was written first, in A.D. 60, around thirty years after Christ's resurrection and ascension. Here, as we have already studied, Paul introduces the concept of the fivefold: apostles, prophets, shepherds, teachers, and evangelists. Therefore, this is how we should set ourselves up, making sure that our priority is these five functioning well in our midst.

Assuming later dates for Paul's "Pastoral Epistles" (which most contemporary scholars now prefer), the letters to Timothy and Titus come another five years later in the growth of the church. Here we receive the concept of elders and deacons, indicating that Paul now recognized a need for a sliding scale of maturity within the already established fivefold leadership. We can therefore have established prophets with a senior leadership function, and emerging prophets growing in practical service.

Most of our modern churches started out of this chronological order and had eldership and a deaconate (or a leadership team and a practical team), complete with measurements of character but lacking measurements of specific fivefold call. And we didn't question this error of omission for years!

I propose that the biblical order is to have fivefold offices holding the senior, governmental roles. In turn, they each lead and run their own teams according to fivefold anointing, with deacons or deputies who minster and practically support these five anointings that reflect Jesus. In other words, you shouldn't just aim to have *one* prophet in a church, you have a senior prophet and teams of prophetic types growing under them. You don't just have *one* teacher in a church, you have a senior teacher and teams of teaching types growing under them. You don't just have *one* apostle in a church, you have a senior apostle and teams of apostolic types growing under them. And so on. This biblical structure allows for serious replication and discipleship, a release of people into the calls on a level that we rarely see.

> You shouldn't just have one prophet in a church; you have a senior prophet and teams of prophetic types growing under them.

Sadly, I think many senior leaders are chosen on their ability to look good rather than raw authenticity. We prefer our leaders to have an air of perfection rather than having a testimony of transformation, and so we set them up to fail by not wanting a connected-heart genuineness but instead valuing a polished exterior. (Not that I am suggesting that we bare our souls to everyone; neither am I demeaning great communication skills—but I suspect that we like our leadership slightly "dehumanized" in an elite way, and not too much like us in our raw humanity. This always robs God of the power of the testimony of redemption.)

We should choose our leaders according to anointing and character—the character that doesn't just look good on the outside but the character that points to a life transformed. Then they will replicate, equip, and release into the lives of deacons and the rest of the body of Christ. The fact that they already know that they have been forgiven, transformed, and set free means that they really value the setting free of everyone. We must require leaders who are fully dependent on grace and who can replicate grace. In other words, this biblical framework requires the people who lead in the most senior places to be more than "professional Christians" or "Church CEOs."

How Easy Is It to Change a Church Culture?

A Word to Leaders

The functions found in the Scriptures that we have unpacked above should give us insight into how Jesus builds a successful church. Most of us probably must admit that our current church and leadership models have been built, at best, foolishly. At worst we have built unbiblically. The future viability of the western church is hanging on our ability to apply a truth that better reflects Jesus back into our structures. I believe that it will take outlandish bravery and courage to reframe church to the degree that is required. This is not a mere matter of reimagining, modernizing, or making our churches more "contemporary" and "relevant," but instead must be born out of a desperation to abandon our own ways in light of the fivefold reality that has always been there in Scripture. This will change how we lead, how we think of ourselves in leadership, and will deeply challenge all that we have known. This is not a truth shift; it is a mindset shift. A full appreciation of biblical church structure will unleash enormous power back to the church and will awaken a new potential in her.

Change is hard. *"And no one after drinking old wine wants the new, for they say, 'The old is better'"* (Luke 5:39 NIV). We are wired to like our old traditions, which means that radical transformation is painful. It takes a level of submission that most never attain, and a level of courage that eludes the majority. The wrestle of total death to self and death to what we previously built requires a brokenness that we don't like.

The thought of killing our familiar, man-made traditions makes us catch our breath. We want to cry out to God, "Lord, can't You just work within what we have built? Can't You take account of the history of this movement? Can't You update it to its former glory, Jesus? God, can't You just see our former glory and place in the world and get on with blessing us right now? Send revival God—we'll manage it with this structure that we've already got in place!"

> **The wrestle of total death to self and death to what we previously built requires a brokenness that we don't like.**

But the Lord replies to us with words like, "You want Me to pour new wine into an old wineskin? Really? How do you think that would go? You want Me to put a new weight of My glory into a structure that is not what I asked you to build?" *"I am the Alpha and the Omega, the First and the Last, the Beginning and the End,"* declares Jesus in verse 13 of Revelation 22. We love the *Alpha* portion of the Lord, who begins a new thing, more than we like the *Omega* version of God, who ends things and brings closure. We forget that it can be as glorious to finish something and to see it die as it is to birth a new thing!

But let's be honest, simply massaging the edges of our frameworks and making little tweaks to our lives is an easier ride. Just working within the existing systems and structures takes less bravery than seeing and acknowledging when their time is over. We are so in love with ourselves and our projects (our "babies"), and so we birth and build self-protecting, self-promoting organizations and maintain them even into decline. We have lost the wild, the radical, the revolutionary—and the biblical—and exchanged it all for a type of slow death that we prefer, because it is familiar, tame, and very controlled.

The ancient Stoic philosopher Epictetus once wrote, "It is impossible for a man to learn what he already thinks he knows."[4] Adding to this thought, Upton Sinclair, the Pulitzer Prize-winning author, warned, "It is difficult to get a man to understand something when his salary depends upon him not understanding it."[5] Applying these two maxims to the church, we could summarize them as saying, "Those who are steeped in tradition, or those who are paid to maintain an existing system, will find it very difficult to embrace change."

At this time, the Lord is taking many leaders into what will become known as "The Season of Resignations and Retirements." Even for those who knew what it was to steward previous moves of God, they too will be released from current positions. This is not a statement of their failure but is instead an acknowledgement that they need to be repositioned—because it is not easy for everyone to shift into apostolic-and-prophetic-building mode.

Therefore, expect many "suddenly" movements of God (and we've already seen some since I began writing this book), in which those who have not been able to keep pace will find themselves out of their current leadership roles. For others, God will come as judge to those leaders who squandered the legacy of the church by teaching people to please themselves rather than bringing up their children in the trembling fear of God. God is measuring church leadership now. It was the same in the days of the prophet Zechariah, when God sent angels to measure, and in that moment of weighing and testing He was looking for the places that He could put His glory. God was looking for those He could protect with a wall of fire—those who qualified because they had yielded to the principles of heaven (see Zechariah 2:1-13).

For those of you who remain in position, work with where you are; start over with biblical models from the foundations. Be brave. Have conversations. Spend hours in dialogue, discussing what your church could become. Allow the current visions that you might have to be ripped up and replaced by God. Pull your people into an understanding that complete restructuring may be the only option that you have! It is a turning of the church, and time for her to be what she should be. Get excited that you are alive at this pivotal point in history! God knew that you needed to be birthed right now, because there is something special in you that is required at this change-point in the history of the people of God. The Kingdom of God is in building mode, and God shall be seen as the *Master Craftsman* once again. Take time to repent because we are eating what we have sown; we are in the consequences of the decisions that we have taken in our history.

The Spirit of the Lord says, "The delight of responsibility will come back onto you for leading a new expression of church, and I will be with you as you relearn your function."

Prayer

> *Jesus, have mercy on us for our self-serving ways. Forgive us where we have assumed that our own structures and traditions are the perfect way, and for not being more biblically inquisitive.*
>
> *In the name of Jesus, I release to you the anointing for apostolic building—that you may now know what to do in this hour. And I release building blueprints into your hands, in Jesus' name. Amen.*

JESUS IN US ALL

What about you? Where do you fit in to all of this? Let's return to Ephesians 4: *"But to each one of us grace has been given as Christ apportioned it"* (Ephesians 4:7 NIV). This sentence (which of course precedes the release of apostles, prophets, shepherds, and teachers a few verses later), literally means that grace has been given to each and every believer. It is a deeply radicalizing verse that has huge ramifications, not just for how we think about leadership, but also how we think about everyone in the church. Apostle Paul is describing a team in which everyone comes to the table with their gifts and contributes to the ongoing development of the body.

Around five years prior to this, Paul had first communicated his thoughts on this to the church in Corinth:

> *Now you are the body of Christ, and each one of you is a part of it. And God has placed in the church first of all apostles, second prophets, third teachers, then miracles, then gifts of healing, of helping, of guidance, and of different kinds of tongues. Are all apostles? Are*

all prophets? Are all teachers? Do all work miracles? Do all have gifts of healing? Do all speak in tongues? Do all interpret? Now eagerly desire the greater gifts. And yet I will show you the most excellent way (1 Corinthians 12:27-31 NIV).

Are all prophets? Obviously not. Everyone has a gifting that reflects Jesus, but not everyone has maturity or leadership function. Everyone is gifted, but not all leaders carry an office call on their life. Nonetheless, everyone who is saved has Jesus in them; everyone has *all* of who Jesus is in them. He didn't give Himself in pieces—He never said, "You can only get this little bit of Me!" We are *all* carrying *all* the aspects of Jesus (though much may be in latent form)! We tend to lean toward displaying only one or two key gifts or anointings, but we still have the capability to understand one another—even if we don't have a portion in us activated that

> The wrestle of total death to self and death to what we previously built requires a brokenness that we don't like.

another person *does* has activated. It is a lie of the enemy that we can't understand each other or that we're too different to work together.

Because Jesus is *wholly* in all of us, I, Emma, can say that I am a prophet and apostle in my specific office, but also, in addition to this, I can lean into evangelistic grace when a soul needs to be saved, or lean into shepherding grace when nurturing is required. That doesn't make me an evangelist or a shepherd. In the same way, no one can therefore complain that "I can't prophesy!" or,

"I can't look after people!" or, "I can't win a soul for Jesus!" or, "I can't understand Scripture!" Jesus is in you, and you can always lean into prophetic grace, shepherding grace, evangelistic grace, teaching grace, and apostolic grace. This makes our goal as leaders to release what is *already in* people; to find the gold and pull it up into focus rather than trying to *put something in*.

STEWARDING YOUR ANOINTING

How do you get started? As the infant New Testament church began to grow, the twelve disciples had to quell expectations that they would be serving tables for the widows. You can really feel the strain in Acts 6 as the young leaders began to wrestle with getting the organizational structure correct in order to steward growth! This passage gives us an insight into the processes of growth, mismanagement of growth, the resulting frustration and infighting, brave conversations, suggested solutions, and realigning actions—resulting in promotions and the sharing of responsibilities. These facets of life should be normal for us all. Managing decline is challenging enough, but managing growth will always require significant restructuring. The church is about to manage unprecedented growth as we step into the days of harvest in the earth.

> The church is about to manage unprecedented growth as we step into the days of harvest in the earth.

The apostles didn't disregard the need for the ministry, but they came into a self-awareness about their anointing—what they carried and where it needed to be spent for the blessing of all. Like them, you must learn the moments when you will need to engage and when you will need to disengage. Proper management of your anointing is a big deal. Many are not seeing the kind of breakthrough that God has for them because they have not been proper stewards of themselves.

One of the biblical principles that we learn from the "Parable of the Talents" (see Matthew 25:14-30) is that you must use well what you have first been given—your anointing, your office, your call, your family. You must not dig a hole and hide your anointing, gift, or office. You must not pretend you don't have a call, or gifts, and partner with some sort of peculiar false humility. Neither do you dress them up or dress them down, overstating or understating what God has put within you.

The Kingdom of God works so incredibly because we have a heavenly Father who is always looking to release more and more to us. However, if—for example—you have an apostle who is constantly looking at the shepherding issues in a church, this a back-door way of them communicating to Heaven that they are not ready for the greater authority in the apostolic that God wants to give them. Then everyone gets stuck!

Prophets, something has to rise up in you that makes you declare, "I know how God made me and I take ownership of my prophetic call. I fully dress myself in the clothes of a prophet that I have been given, and I receive this call *in its entirety*."

God wants to blow through your diary and remove all that your hands touch that does not have His favor, and all that you have minimal expertise in or a call to. Get rid of false responsibility and of being a "doormat" that people walk all over because you have not displayed your gifts. Stop any partnership with unsanctified mercy and false compassion, where you are putting time energy, mercy, and sympathetic effort into things that God is not putting His time, energy, and mercy on in this moment. You cannot fix what you do not have an anointing to fix!

When you and your running mates truly get hold of this, it will be radically liberating for you. My father, Pastor John Hansford, is a shepherd-teacher and has retired to our city to work with our ministry. This means that I do not have to think about shepherding as a dominant, repetitive, mental exercise. Likewise, my father does not have to do mind gymnastics to figure out how an apostle or prophet would think in a situation. In turn, our church congregation understands and knows who they would go to if they needed a prophetic word, and who they would go to if they wanted to be nurtured. You will *never* be all things to all people, and if you try, you will lose your well-being and wear yourself out.

> "I take ownership of my prophetic call. I fully dress myself in the clothes of a prophet that I have been given, and I receive this call *in its entirety*."

In terms of our actual meeting or service structure, I am free to lead in wild, prophetic activations—as the Spirit leads—and if all that craziness makes some people feel uncomfortable, they know they can probably ride it out, because next week there will be a shepherd-teacher on the platform who will help everyone to feel grounded again. This has led to happier—and more extreme—versions of ourselves, in which we are all totally empowered to steward the fullness of our call and there are more peaceful and joyful people around us who know how to make a right with-drawal from each of us, according to our anointings.

ACTIVATION

Right now, call to God and ask Him to help you steward your anointing. With the Spirit's help, draw up a list of some of the areas you find yourself ministering in or that you have been eager to minister in. Ask Him if these really are actually the areas that you are anointed in. Listen to what He says and pray about it. You might need to discuss your list and pray over it with a good friend who can speak boldly into your life because sometimes those who know us well can see things in us that we are blind to. Repent to God of holding on to things that were not yours to carry—and for not picking up those things that were your call. Be prepared for some doors to open and others to slam shut.

CHAPTER 6

Becoming a Prophet

HOW DO YOU know if you are a prophet? Let's work through a checklist together and get a feel for what the office of prophet entails.

The Criteria for Becoming a Prophet

1. Prophets must be recommended by those who know them. This means that there must be a track record of words as well as relationships that work. Someone with seniority must be able to have measured you over time and found you to be reliable in stewarding the voice of God.

2. Those in the office of prophet must understand their relationship with the other calls and anointings, and, having done so, will know and recognize when prophecy is required—and, equally importantly, when it is not. Prophecy is not the solution to every problem! It is part of the jigsaw puzzle of the family of God.

3. Mature prophets must be consistent. You cannot ebb and flow in investing in relationships. You must be able to take responsibility for your words and actions because you cannot expect people to believe that you've heard from God if there has not been a solid reliability from you. This means that you know when to turn up frequently and faithfully, both in your daily devotions and in the life of the church.

4. No "Lone Rangers"! If you are going to carry the voice of God, you must be accountable and completely open to sharpening from leaders, even if it stings.

5. Prophets must be self-aware. This is important because prophetic words can be so life-changing to those who hear them that the prophet needs to know how to choose things such as tone of voice, body language, and giving appropriate timings so that the voice of God can be best received.

6. Prophets will have measurable authority. By the very nature of their call, prophets carry spiritual authority. They don't just speak things, they shift things! As a result, there will be measurable, manifest changes in lives and situations because a prophet spoke.[1]

7. Those who are in the office of prophet must be of excellent character.

8. They must be disciplined and able to take responsibility. Some words can be so strong that the giver

of the revelation must be accountable for the relational shifting and challenges that happen as a result. This means not running away or retreating into a cave when the going gets tough. Once you learn this, God will trust you with more weighty words because you will have a track record of doing your duty and sticking around to work things out with people.

9. Prophets must be comfortable with the spiritual/supernatural rather than looking for the spectacular.

10. Those with the prophet's call will instinctively spend time in the business of hearing God's strategy for cities, nations, and groups of people.

11. They will have capability in dealing with leaders who, in turn, shape nations.

12. Prophets will be able to express words of correction and direction without rudeness or aggression.

13. They will be able to navigate the strange and peculiar without discrediting Jesus Christ. For example, God once asked me to pour anointing oil inside a husband and wife's purse. Initially it seemed incredibly disrespectful to soak the leather and potentially ruin it! They were in church leadership, struggling financially, and God wanted to turn their finances around through a prophetic act. The Lord then said to decree that by the same time the following week they would have £10,000 in their bank account, and after that significant financial

breakthrough. By the following week they had indeed received a gift of £10,000 and breakthrough in home ownership!

Only God chooses who is a prophet. No one can arbitrarily call you into the office of prophet and decide that you are one. We can recognize the anointing and call on each other, and we can clarify that someone has the office of the prophet, but we cannot make you a prophet. We can raise and train you—and in fact you do have a responsibility to develop your calling—but you are born as a prophet and birthed into a vocation by God alone.

Many experienced prophets believe that it takes a minimum of fourteen years for a person to develop into a mature, usable prophet—that's fourteen years *after* the first moment that they realized they were called. This time frame is based on King David's life, when it was fourteen years from his anointing as king to his ascension to the throne. Certainly, it takes many, many years for the full weight and governmental anointing of a prophet to sit on one's shoulders in a measurably useful way. I am often asked if this concept can be truncated, accelerated, or fast-tracked. But would you want someone speaking into the destiny of nations who hadn't submitted to the due process of God? It takes years to become mature in the call.

> **It takes years to become mature in the call.**

By virtue of being chosen by God to be a prophet, you do not have the *gift* of prophecy; rather, *you* are the gift. To *minister* in prophecy is a gift. To be a prophet is a *calling*. The call is not something you *do*; it is something you *are*. This distinction must be clearly understood because you do not switch the office of the prophet on and off. Therefore, you will learn through watching a prophet's life; each and every prophet should be living a story, living the revelation of God. Their life is always a sign, and by watching how they live you ought to be impacted by the parables their life displays of what God is saying today.

Learn to see your life as a story. You are telling the world about what God is saying. If you miss this, then you will spend much of your life in painful conjectures, mentally trying to ascertain why your life is as it is! Learn to ask the question, "Lord, what story are You telling people through what I have to live through?" Very often you are equipped to walk through things that are not easy to bear, just so that others might learn from your journey. Learn to take your eyes off yourself and ask prophetic questions like, "Father, what do You need displayed in the earth through me?" You are not here just to be a spokesperson on behalf of the divine. Much more than that, you are to model the full spectrum of how God communicates—and God is an incredible storyteller!

> The call of a prophet is not something you do; it is something you are. You don't have the gift—you are the gift.

Hosea is perhaps the prime biblical example of this. He was called by God to marry the prostitute, Gomer. He had to model the unfaithfulness of Israel to her God, painfully and repetitively, through the drama of his own personal journey as a husband to a publicly unfaithful wife. He walked through the utter rejection of

Gomer and even had to buy her back from other lovers in order to take her back into his bed.

Activation

Take some time with Jesus to review your life and ask Him to show you when your life was a story that was delivering a prophetic message. This most likely means that you will go back through hard memories of some tough, perhaps painful times. However, if you allow Him to show you what He was doing, you will not regret it. Instead, you will find that you have a message of thanksgiving—that God trusted you with His message.

MY OWN STORY

Some years ago, David and I and our three children found ourselves homeless. We had walked into what you might call a "perfect storm" of God. The initial instinct in this situation might have been to bind the devil and call on an immediate Holy Spirit solution. However, at that time we felt no liberty to pray anything other than, "Teach us what we need to learn so we don't go round this mountain again, and let our lives tell the story that You want seen in Scotland." We were rescued by some friends and ended up living in their attic. Ten of us shared one bathroom, my boys shared a bed, and David and I and Jessica (our daughter) shared another bed.

We thought that this learning journey would last, at best, a few weeks and, at most, a couple of months, but how wrong we were! In the end we lived in what was a ridiculous situation for just over seven months. There was a mammoth amount of grace and ease, and we all look back on it as one of our best adventures in God, although it did put our extended family members through the wringer emotionally as they watched us from afar.

Predominantly we were telling a story of the literal and metaphorical homelessness of the prophets in the British Isles at the time, and of the lack of receptivity in hearts and minds to giving them a place of belonging. It was a screaming sign of the rejection of the prophets in the land.

Often when you're going through something quite personal you don't have the stomach to share it with other people, and the natural instinct is to keep it to yourself. It's usual to want to wait until it is all over to turn the story into a testimony. However, in this case God demanded that we share the story of our homelessness, blow by blow, as we were walking through each stage of it. This was deeply uncomfortable, but we knew that if we did not share, what would have been the point of the journey? God needed it to be seen and for it to bring provocation, month after month after month.

(As a side note, one day I was standing in the school playground at pick-up time, when one of the other non-Christian mums asked me, "Are you still living with your friends? Do you still not have a house?" I immediately felt embarrassed and challenged that my God might not look good because of my situation. However, as I turned to reply, "Yes, we are still there," she interjected, "You only ever speak of it as being a good experience. You Christians must really love each other!" God was telling another, layered story with our lives, one that we had not even recognized ourselves.)

David's and my story continued, and we did eventually move into a rented house. This was a wonderful blessing—but it was not *ownership*. When I first sat down to draft this chapter of this book, I wrote of how I had the sense that our lives will continue to tell a story of how the prophets are received in the British Isles and that when we eventually own a home, it will be a sign of prophets truly possessing their possessions and being received and integrated into the fabric of the people of God in this land. Now, as I finalize this book, I am pleased to add that we *have* now purchased a home, made possible by miraculous gifts from beautiful supporters of our family from all over the world! This is a sign!

Your story continues also, and in the right time your life, woven together with the story that God is telling in the nations, will say all that God needs said through it.

THE STORY OF A CALL

Not only do prophets live revelation, but they must also know they are called by God and have a story of their own call. Many of the prophets in Scripture have a report of how they came into the role. For example, Samuel in the temple with Eli knew of his dedication to the Lord and of hearing His voice from very early childhood (see 1 Samuel 3). Jeremiah while still a teenager understood the story of being known and chosen by God before he was formed (see Jeremiah 1:5). Amos also had a moment of receiving his call:

> *Amos answered Amaziah, "I was neither a prophet nor the son of a prophet, but I was a shepherd, and I also took care of sycamore-fig trees. But the Lord took me from tending the flock and said to me, 'Go, prophesy to my people Israel'"* (Amos 7:14-15 NIV).

I love Amos' complete ignorance of his call into the office of prophet until later in his life. Seemingly unaware of his ability to steward revelation, he had shepherding skills and his life was going in a totally different direction. Now there is a book of the Bible named after him!

When Isaiah saw the Lord in Isaiah 6, there was a major shift in his call. John the Baptist leapt in the womb and had prophetic words before his birth, ordering his steps. After hands were laid on Barnabas in Acts 13, he totally shifted gear in anointing.

What is the story of your call? If you haven't yet had one and are feeling a little like Amos the shepherd, ask God to make His call on your life obvious through confirming signs and wonders. We often need a moment of undeniable certainty to a call, something to look back on when the "screaming moments" come and when criticism is raised against you or demonic attack intensifies. It's quite common in ministerial circles to hear leaders joke of repetitively handing in their notice to quit to God. Some even confess to quitting every Monday morning after the struggles of Sunday services! When you have tested and approved your call and you know beyond any reasonable doubt that God requires your life to steward revelation, you will have won the longevity and security that will hold you in the days when men, demons, and sometimes even your own heart doubt your role. The testimony of a call becomes a vitally important anchor moment, securing your stability amidst opposition for years.

> **The testimony of a call becomes a vitally important anchor moment, securing your stability amidst opposition for years.**

I find this to be especially true when the Lord requires me to bring words that are not easy—for example, where sin must be faced in the life of a leader or course corrections must be spoken. In these moments you can lean into God, pray for wisdom, and whisper to yourself that He has called you and you are not here for a popularity contest. When you can whisper a remembrance of your call to your heart, it will give you great courage to keep living as a prophet.

CHAPTER 7

What Are Prophets Like?

Prophets Are Strange and Intense

Prophets are strange. Perhaps they are the most peculiar of all the anointings God gives. Even many years into this journey I still laugh at the weird things God asks us to do, like chasing a demonic octopus down the main street in Glasgow, and very publicly commanding it to leave the city! The thousands passing by must have thought that we were out of our minds. Let's spend some time looking at the personality of the prophet so we can better understand ourselves in all our strangeness.

Prophets speak with intensity because of what they have seen. Revelation immediately presses on their emotions; they feel it deeply. Therefore, you rarely hear them speak in shades of gray—it's nearly always either black or white—because when you have beheld the glory of God or have heard Him speak, you dare not dilute it. Revelation often comes out in extreme language, like with Ezekiel, who is rich in imagery about eyes, wings, wheels within wheels, burning glory, rushing wind, crashing glory noises, and God seated on a throne outside the circle of the earth.

Isaiah paints the picture of Jesus in pain and in a bloodied mess—consider the intensity of his words, "by His stripes we are healed" and "the punishment was upon His shoulders," which lead us into almost hearing the lashes of a whip as the prophet unpacks what he has seen.

John the Revelator recounts Jesus' face shining like the sun in its noonday brilliance, with a voice like many waters. He's glowing as hot metal, and you can sense John's shock at his vision of Jesus being seen with a two-edged sword in His mouth. No wonder he fell down as if dead!

Prophets Are Extreme

Prophetic revelation has a feeling; it marks you. God grabs the attention of the prophet by not just pulling them into an auditory experience with His voice alone, but by pulling them into a complete, whole-body encounter with His words, His ways, His emotions, and with divine purity. Remember that Jeremiah describes God's words as "fire shut up in his bones" (see Jeremiah 20:9). This leads to a certain sort of urgent communication. The prophet often wants to unburden themselves of the weight of the revelation they are carrying, and so you commonly hear them say things like, "The time is now!" or "We must act immediately!"

> **Prophets are easily bored, action oriented, like speed, and feel deeply and strongly.**

Friends with prophetic grace usually live life between two opposite mindsets: either it's all wonderful, or it's all awful—they are happy in extremes! Born ready, they are easily bored and prefer fast-paced change. They are action oriented and are made with a liking for speed because they need to handle the urgent fact that it's imperative for people to change and get holy before it's too late! They feel deeply and strongly.

Prophets are required to disturb, agitate, and question. Never content with the status quo, they rock the boat, pester, and irritate, until everyone pays attention to whatever aspects of their lives are not reflecting God. Because of their unrelenting sense of needing to get people ready for what's coming, or to change, or to get transformed, they make themselves hard to take, on occasion, and are often marginalized—at best. At worst, they are killed.

PROPHETS ARE WIRED FOR JUSTICE AND RIGHTEOUSNESS

Prophetic people are wired for justice and righteousness. When these strong emotions are mishandled, they can stray into heavy-handed judgment and criticism very easily. Their internal injustice monitors can go at "warp speed" in moments, making them prone to overreact. Therefore, they must remember to take several steps back on some occasions, allowing time to review and weigh situations, especially when they are aware of a super-strong emotion rising in them. Do you remember Jonah

> Prophetic people are wired for justice and righteousness but can stray into heavy-handed judgment and criticism very easily.

sitting down grumpily, in emotional turmoil, during chapter 4 of his story? It is a brilliant study of a moody, bad-tempered prophet, who is not happy that God is compassionate about Nineveh. Jonah's inability to regulate his own emotional response temporarily casts him into the belly of a fish and into a judgment story of his own making.

Similarly, with Elisha we see a man who has great authority misuse it when he perceives an injustice—the criticism against his personal appearance. In 2 Kings 2, a group of young boys tease him for his baldness. Elisha's sense of injustice boils over into judgment and he calls down two female bears to maul to death those who made fun of him. Forty-two children died over his reaction to his disrespected appearance.

Any reading of this story is not easy. If we feel that Elisha was completely justified in his death order over the teenagers, we land in a place where hatred, mockery, and dishonor of God's prophets is serious enough to be life limiting. To jeer at a prophet was to insult God. Whichever way we read this passage, it should at least help us understand the extremes of the prophetic personality and the life they are called to. Let us use this example to be conscious of why we read so much from certain prophetic groups today about judgment (often to unhelpful extremes) whose intolerance silos them away and stops them from being salt and light on the earth.

Prophets Are Dramatic

Prophets are happy with drama. Nathan the prophet, whom we find in 2 Samuel 12, weaves together a highly elaborate and emotionally heart-wrenching allegory about a man stealing a sheep in order to rebuke King David for his taking of Bathsheba as his own wife (and in the process effectively murdering her husband). This is much more of an embellished solo drama than a straightforward, didactic, prophetic word.

In the New Testament, Agabus the prophet appears and ties himself up with Paul's belt to dramatically illustrate the important point that he wants to make. He certainly made an impression on Luke, who records it in Acts 21. Back in the Old, Samuel and his company of prophets are described as noisily coming down the mountain in a big procession, banging drums, and playing instruments (see 1 Samuel 10:5). In Ezekiel 4, the prophet was told to lie on his side for weeks to make a point: 390 days on his left side, 40 days on his right. Isaiah went even further—he did his stint *naked* and preached that way for three years! (See Isaiah 20.) Ezekiel did have a dramatic limit—he drew the line at cooking his food over human excrement! (See Ezekiel 4.)

If you like strange and cutting-edge clothes, you're in good company!

Jeremiah hid his underwear under a rock for a long time before going back to retrieve it. He then wore it, full of holes, to make an eye-catching statement about the people's lack of intimacy with God (see Jeremiah 13). John the Baptizer was happy in clothing that challenged the status quo, complemented by a diet that is as much noteworthy as it is stomach-churning! *"John's clothes were made of camel's hair, and he had a leather belt around his waist. His food was locusts and wild honey"* (Matthew 3:4 NIV).

In 2 Kings 1, Elijah is described physically as being a man with a "garment" of hair and a leather belt. The original Hebrew text gives a sense of disheveled hair—literally meaning "a lord of hair." According to one commentator, this reference might have been about the length of his hair and beard, his hirsute skin, or to a hairy cloak or mantle.[1] A hairy mantle was a mark of the prophetic office from Elijah down through the years until at least John the Baptizer. So, if you like strange and cutting-edge clothes, you're probably in good biblical company.

Lying for Dramatic Effect: The 1 Kings 20 Showman!

An incredible story in 1 Kings 20 features a unique brand of prophetic showmanship. Israel, led by King Ahab, found itself under repeated attack from the king of Aram and a large coalition of other nations. In the passage, an unnamed prophet of God comes to Ahab and prophesies not only successive victories for Israel but also the terms and conditions for how those wins would be achieved. However, evil King Ahab wrongly spares the lives of his royal enemies, despite exacting a great military victory over them.

> With shrewd planning and dramatic portrayal, the prophet delivers the word of the Lord.

Seeking to correct King Ahab, the prophet gets his friend to bash him on the head, so that he looks bloodied and bruised. The prophet then lies by the roadside, wrapped in bandages and waiting for King Ahab to drive past. (Do read the full chapter in the Bible, it is even wilder—including lions—than this shortened version.)

Ahab duly stops and asks him how he has been wounded. The prophet lies (and this is *not* the only time in Scripture that a prophet lies for effect), making up a story about losing a prisoner he was supposed to guard with his life. Ahab is about to sentence him to death for being a useless guard when the prophet leaps up, rips off his disguise, and with great mastery of delivery says, "It's me, King Ahab! Because you let out of your hands the man God vowed to destroy, your life will be for his life!" Thus, with shrewd planning and dramatic portrayal, the prophet delivers the word of the Lord.

However, prophets, be careful to use your drama only with heavenly permission and not with emotive manipulation to get your own way. If you live over-dramatically—and this can be the defining weakness of a prophet—you are hard to take seriously when you really do need to impactfully display a word of the Lord.

Activation

Ask the Lord to show you the place of storytelling and dramatic presentations in your life, where theater, tragedy, parable, and role play could be part of your biblically legitimate "toolbox." Remember that melodrama is not helpful and if you always live in drama then you will rob yourself of rest, quickly getting yourself out of the timings of God.

Prayer

> *I release you into the rhythms of God and call you, in Jesus' name, into divinely led cycles of peace and drama, rest and action. In the name of Jesus, I speak an inner security into your hope of salvation and*

into your call, so that you may be settled internally— and from that inner stability have the wisdom of God to know the right actions in every moment that revelation is required. Amen.

PROPHETS ARE COVENANT GUARDIANS

Prophets have one driving motivation that underpins all that they do. Prophets are guardians of the people's covenant relationship with Yahweh. They are continually moved to get people to respond rightly to Almighty God. This means they are wired to love holiness and everything that pleases the Lord. Called to maintain faithfulness to God, prophets become aware of His heart. Theirs is an unending job of motivating a people to change and live faithfully in light of the future to come. Therefore, conversations about prayer, fasting, and intense spiritual disciplines seem very normal to them.

When they are not in full-time ministry, prophets are often found in issues of justice, environmental responsibilities, reforming systems, politics and government, the military, stewardship, and involved in the exposure of wrongdoing. Because their eyes cast into the future, they are usually present-future oriented, not often dwelling on the past. As prophets guard the covenant relationship with God, they are instinctively principled and desiring of truthfulness and authenticity. When they go wrong, they are the anarchists and the hackers.

> **Prophets are guardians of the people's covenant relationship with Yahweh.**

They are the wild extremes of society, who are very happy to fight when the situation requires it. Occasionally they speak too mystically for anyone to understand or too determinedly for anyone to receive! Eugene Peterson, author of *The Message*, summed up prophets beautifully when he wrote:

> The work of the prophet is to call people to live well, to live rightly...But it is more than a call to say something, it is a call to live out the message. The prophet must be what he or she says.
>
> ...A prophet lets people know who God is and what he is like, what he says and what he is doing. A prophet wakes us up from our sleepy complacency so that we see the great and stunning drama that is our existence, and then pushes us onto the stage playing our parts whether we think we are ready or not. A prophet angers us by rejecting our euphemisms and ripping off our disguises, then dragging our heartless attitudes and selfish motives out into the open where everyone sees them for what they are. A prophet makes everything and everyone seem significant and important—important because God made it, or him, or her. A prophet makes it difficult to continue with a sloppy or selfish life.[2]

Mature prophets bring a standard that affects the atmosphere in the room—a standard that God's voice *must* be heard, and that faithfulness to Him and His presence in all decisions must not be lost. God gives prophetic people the temperament and personality that can carry revelation. But watch out! Because of the provocative nature of their call, if everyone likes a prophetic person, they are probably doing life wrong!

If you have capped yourself to be accepted or dumbed down your anointing and call, if you have lost your extremeness, taming yourself for men rather than embracing your call before God and man—*now* is the moment to deal with it!

ACTIVATION

You were not made to be universally applauded; you were made to be a challenge to all that is not holy. Take a moment to close your eyes and ask Jesus to pull off your life every piece of grave clothes that you are wrapped in that brings death to who God wants you to be.

Allow the burning fire of God to reignite you and burn you into all He needs you to be.

CHAPTER 8

THE TYPES OF PROPHETS

NOW THAT WE have considered the overarching sense of what a prophet is and what prophets are like, let's drill down into some differing specializations within the prophetic anointing. It is important that each prophet knows their strengths, their remit, and their personal boundaries. No two prophets are identical. Each person's remit as a prophet is shaped by how trustworthy they have become and their personal history with God. Therefore, the constant cry from our hearts should be, "Lord, make me trustworthy with Your voice, and with the revelation You have given into my hands." This is a constant prayer that should put us on our knees in reverential fear in order that we might be able to steward the next levels of revelation He wants issued in the earth. It is this prayer that personally makes me shake because I have become increasingly aware of the cost of

> The constant cry from our hearts should be, "Lord, make me trustworthy with Your voice, and with the revelation You have given into my hands."

stewarding new levels of revelation. At the same time, His voice is the sweetest thing in my life. That He would trust me, that He would trust you, surely is worthy of a holy trembling.

TWO OPERATIONAL REMITS: ELIJAH AND MOSES

How will God use you? We generally see two operational preferences within the prophetic, archetypally exemplified by the lives of Elijah and Moses. Elijah was sent to many leaders and many nations. He spoke into Queen Jezebel and Kings Ahab and Ahaziah of Israel and King Jehoram of Judah, meaning that he thought outside of the boundaries of one tribe or place. Moses, on the other hand, was sent to one people, and he led them where they needed to go.

Elijah was wired for new opportunities, seeking to set the agenda and activity of the interaction he had with the prophets of Baal (see 1 Kings 18). He was searching for the creative expressions of God and the fresh ways that He wanted to be seen. Conversely, Moses-style prophets prefer working through the existing *ecclesia* (church). Remember that Moses, in Exodus 18, restructured how the people were locally governed and selected judges for the people.

> **Elijah prophets focus on nations and prefer short term, high risk, and new. They are the often-misunderstood agents of change.**

Elijah Prophets

Elijah prophets love wide open frontiers. They resist bureaucratic constraints; they extend the voice of God beyond the church. They are exploratory and *founding* (meaning they give foundational words that begin new things) as they pioneer the new. Elijah prophets love cross-cultural interactions relating to different tribes. They are culturally savvy and are interested in what is going on within a nation (a "national prophet"). They are outward looking, which becomes greatly challenging if this anointing runs a church. This is because their focus is rarely the people right in front of them in a consistent, single locality. Yet at the same time they must still learn to be rooted somewhere. Elijah prophets focus on nations, preferring short-term assignments. High risk delights them; they are "change agents" but are often misunderstood as dissenters because they will always object to what is not right!

Moses Prophets

Moses prophets will remove the barriers that get in the way of being authentic church, mobilizing the church to fulfill its mission and calling. They will bring the voice of God to shift the identity of the church. They are focused on developing people, *re-founding* (making better what is already in place), marshalling and

> Moses prophets focus on developing people, mobilizing the church and what is already there. They are moderate risk agitators who manage change.

activating what is already there. They are intercultural, always seeking to answer the question, "How do the people of this place think and behave?"

They are diplomatically savvy, knowing what to say and how to say it so as not to deliberately offend people. They will lead a people forward with a focus on what is happening inside an organization. Rather than a focus on the nations, they focus on the people of God *for the sake of the nations*. Their assignments are medium to long term; they have a preference for moderate risk and are viewed more as agitators than as dissenters. They are "change managers" rather than "change agents."

ACTIVATION

To help you understand the difference between Elijah and Moses prophets, why not draw up a two-column table, headed "Elijah" and "Moses"? List the differences above under each heading— and see what other examples you can find in Scripture of the difference between Elijah the prophet and Moses the prophet. Which archetype do you feel more drawn to? There's no right or wrong answer! But make sure you are listening to the Holy Spirit and not just making assumptions based on your personality type or romantic preference!

THINGS ELIJAH AND MOSES PROPHETS NEED TO WORK ON

The Moses type of prophet certainly has a "softer" feel than the cut of the Elijah prophet. But there is overlap in being a guardian of the voice of God, speaking in order to architect hope, and being a custodian of truth. There is so much wisdom required for each archetype, and different prayers must be diligently prayed as the strengths and weaknesses of each type are lived out.

Elijah prophets must pray to develop compassion and stay away from the "hit and run" ministry approach, where you turn up and drop vocal bombs, only to leave the building as soon as possible! This type of prophet is very easily misunderstood because of their strength. When they have developed maturity and the associated authority, they do change the direction of nations. Therefore, their personal purity must be exemplary, and relational savviness will always need to be worked on. Elijah prophets will often have to lay hands on themselves and ask

> Elijah prophets must not "hit and run," must pursue personal purity, and work on their relational savviness. They will need to develop peace and patience and learn to let God defend their reputation.

for peace in their insides, which get churned up either by coping with rejection or from the irritation at unrighteousness that underpins who they are. They will often need to develop patience with the saints. Elijahs are prone to the dramatic—Elijah himself had moments of real outspokenness in prayer and dialogue with God. For example, his cry of, "Why have you let this woman's son die?" (see 1 Kings 17:20-21), or when he wanted to go out to the wilderness to die (see 1 Kings 19:4).

They must be careful that they don't stoop low into point-scoring against others or self-justification. If this applies to you, learn to let God defend your reputation!

Moses prophets must pray for an ability to be sustained and patient in transitioning the people they have been called to. To double-check if you are a Moses, ask God, "Do I have a transitioning or bridging anointing to move people from one place to another?" If you do, there will be a special grace to faithfully stay, even amid great misunderstanding or frustrations. Moses learns not to lash out. In his early days he had killed an Egyptian in a moment of rage, but as he ages he comes to a place of greater stability. It is in the one moment of striking the rock, when after decades of care, he loses his patience of transitioning people, that God retires him. That one significant overstep and Yahweh will not have him in charge.

This is not supposed to strike an unhealthy fear into our hearts, but rather to sharpen our minds in understanding how God prefers His people to be led. Moses debriefs with God in wonderful conversations:

"God, they are *Your* people."

"No, they are *your* people, Moses!"

God and Moses bat back and forward in sharing a mutual frustration over the waywardness of Israel. The honesty of Moses and of the Lord in their interactions is heartwarming. Almighty God clearly allows the Moses prophet a safe conversational space, which ultimately means that he's less likely to explode in front of the people he's leading.

Moses prophets carry a bridging anointing and must pray to be sustained and patient, resisting the urge to lash out.

It is a real skill to move a people over time, and along the journey Moses types often miss God's bigger picture, become risk averse, lose bravery, and fail to see the long-term vision.

PRAY

Help me, Jesus, to learn to steward the specific anointing that You have given individually to me. I want to be faithful to what You have put in my hands. I am sorry for when I wanted the anointing and call that somebody else had that was never for me.

Help me to be sensitive to know when I am to stay and transition a people group and when I am to be sent and pioneer. In Jesus' name I pray, amen.

CHAPTER 9

The Three Ways
of Revelation

IN ADDITION TO the operational remit of the prophet are three distinct ways that the prophet sources and relays revelation. Let's look at them in turn.

The Nabi Prophet

The Hebrew word meaning "to prophesy" in the Bible is נָבָא naba.[1] Thus, those who prophesied were called נָבִיא nabi ("prophets"), alluding to their style of communication—that they "naba-ed" what they heard from God. *Naba* means "to bubble up, to pour forth, to flow, to have an abundance of words." It's a gush of language—often like a rapid-fire machine gun—and it can be fascinating to watch the speed at which revelation can be uttered. You will often wonder how the prophet is processing the revelation at pace, but you do get used to a symbiotic relationship with the Spirit of God. Experience and practice underpin this in its mature form. You can either speak the words or sing them. We find the word *naba* in the Hebrew texts associated with these prophets: Abraham, Iddo, Zechariah, Asaph, Gad, Amos,

Heman, Habakkuk, Jeduthan, Samuel, Isaiah, Jeremiah, Ezekiel, Daniel, Joel, Obadiah, Jonah, Micah, and Malachi.

Naba prophesying is *not* the ability to say a lot of words for words' sake, like a verbal unstopability, and it's not a raving extrovert who doesn't perceive their word count! No, it is the ability to flow in the words of prophecy that land right at the core of a situation and, like a key unlocks, bring life. They are targeted, specific utterances.[2]

When you *naba* revelation, it is not just your breath that the words are carried on, but also the Holy Spirit carries them and lands them. The *nabi* prophet will have a deep partnership with the Holy Spirit, who gives the utterances. It is a profound fellowshipping with the Spirit that enables this to be unlocked. The Holy Spirit enables a *naba* abundance of words to flow out of you.

It is worth noting that in the Old Testament, God put words in the prophets' mouths; however, in the New Testament, under the New Covenant of Jesus, *words flow from the indwelling Holy Spirit*. In the Old Covenant, prophecy was an *event* because the Holy Spirit did not live inside them, and so prophetic people *received* a word from God. Still today we wrongly sit in this model, crying out for revelation: "God, give me something, anything," waiting for it to possibly hit your receiving dish, "Will God/won't God?" But we have the Holy Spirit inside us, we live under a New Covenant, so we don't need to *receive*; rather, we *perceive* what the Holy Spirit is saying as He communes with our spirit.

> *But whoever is united with the Lord is one with him in spirit* (1 Corinthians 6:17 NIV).

You are already one spirit in Jesus so relax, take a deep breath, and listen. The longer I have prophesied, the more convinced I have become of our utter stuck-ness in old thinking. We set ourselves up to not steward revelation by waiting for it to externally hit us. While we are waiting in error, we miss the joy of continual, conversational relationship that is already happening inside of us. Our dullness to perpetual relationship with the Spirit indwelling us pushes us out of revelatory usefulness, because we are not continually in fellowship! God has to wait until we are ready to bother listening, rather than us being ever ready because of constant dialogue and awareness with what is happening inside of us.

> Our dullness to perpetual relationship with the Spirit indwelling us pushes us out of revelatory usefulness because we are not continually in fellowship!

We should be constantly aware of what the Holy Spirit is doing inside—His voice, His timings, His thinking, His mindset, and His urgency to communicate. When you know Him well, a rapid flow of language seems very normal.

We know from Scriptures, such as the Parable of the Sower (see Matthew 13), that when we *naba* it has an effect like seeding the words inside a person (see 1 Peter 1:23). The Holy Spirit carries the word and plants it within the spirit of the person you are speaking to. Then, when it has been planted, it can grow and change a life.

Some people can look very off-putting when you prophesy over them—their body language is slumped, appearing full of depression and sullenness, and they look like they are chewing a wasp! It is easy (and human) to assume, "Oh, OK, I must prophesy about joy," and get it all wrong. Alternatively, we can get intimidated by their looks and back down. So when you *naba*, you must go past the skin and presentation and prophesy Spirit to spirit. Holy Spirit to human spirit.

We want to be people who prophesy Spirit to spirit, and not flesh to flesh. It should never be a word for their ego. This is why some people in the moment do not understand what you are saying (and why it is important to record words to review later). Because of this, never ask someone whom you're prophesying over a question like, "Does that makes sense?" because it is *not* always going to make sense to them in that moment! When you ask a question like that, you are really asking for the receiver to make you feel good and to pump up your own ego. You must be able to leave a seed to grow and, as it grows, it will take over the space of the weeds (the lies) that they have been believing.

This is why we read 1 Samuel 3:19 that none of *nabi* prophet Samuel's words fell to the ground. They didn't "spill out of him" and land at his feet having no effect! Instead, they must have been carried by a *naba* Holy Spirit flow, flying straight to where they would have an impact. They were "seed words"! I have had many conversations with other prophets regarding this statement that, *"The Lord…let none of Samuel's words fall to the ground."* Does this verse mean that Samuel was absolutely, 100 percent perfect and accurate in every single utterance? Or did God back him up at those times when he got it wrong, in order to protect the reputation of the prophetic, and so made even the wrong things he said to happen? Perhaps this is a question to ask God when we all get to Heaven!

Words that have been *naba*-ed land and are hard to shake off. They resonate and rattle in you, remaining for years as hope for the future. Have you ever had a word that you couldn't shake? It was because a seed was put inside you, and it is growing!

Have you ever had a wrong prophetic seed sown and grown in you and it has done some damage? Let me pray for its removal:

> *In the name of Jesus, I lift and pull from you any wrong seed of revelation that was inaccurately sown into you. Where it grew in error and created false expectation and disappointment, may the healing balm of Jesus soothe your emotions and restore what has been lost. Lord Jesus, I ask that You would whisper now to them personally and reframe their outlook, giving them eyes to see what You really have for them. Thank You, Jesus, that You are the God of exchange—You remove what does us harm and You plant in us what will bless us. Amen.*

Naba Words Lead to Deliverance

When you are in the *naba* flow and are planting a seed, people will occasionally get angry or weep because they have forgotten who God made them to be. You sow revelation, it grows, and it is different from how they have been and are, right in that moment, and this rattles them. This frequently leads to the demonic coming out, just as we prophesy a seed in. The person is

> If a prophet is not involved in deliverance ministry, they will be quenching the full work of the Holy Spirit, who is both a revelator and liberator.

suddenly awakened to God.

Therefore, we must expect to have to do deliverance as part of prophetic ministry. The seeds displace demons or highlight blockages in their life that have prevented the seeds of revelation to fully grow. Therefore, if a prophetic person is not involved in deliverance ministry, they will be quenching the full work of the Holy Spirit, who is both a revelator *and liberator*. When deliverance is what you need, nothing else will work![3]

Healthcare for Nabi Prophets

Nabi prophets are "word smiths." It is a little like turning on a tap when they prophesy. Their great strength is that they are nearly always able to minster. They can connect with the flow of internal Holy Spirit communication relatively quickly. However, this ability to "switch on" revelation carries with it a great danger, if a *nabi* is not careful. They can fall into prophesying without feeling anything, emotionally disconnected, prophesying without being interested in the person in front of them. Words will pour out and yet they can write a shopping list in the back of their minds at the same time, mentally distracted because they have tuned into the words of God but not the emotions of God. It is therefore important for *nabi* prophets to continually be working on their heart-health issues, just because of how the desire to emotionally shut down or over-withdraw is so strong in this group of prophetic types.

A "best practice" for *nabi* prophets is to engage for lengthy periods in adoring worship before ministering. This will connect them to God and help them to be aware of how they feel—and to be asking God how He feels.

THE SEER PROPHET

> *And when David arose in the morning, the word of the Lord came to the prophet Gad, David's seer, saying…* (2 Samuel 24:11 ESV).
>
> *As for the events of King David's reign, from beginning to end, they are written in the records of Samuel the seer, the records of Nathan the prophet and the records of Gad the seer* (1 Chronicles 29:29 NIV).

Another type of prophet in the Bible is the *seer*. *Seer* is the English translation of two Hebrew words, רֹאֶה (*ro-eh*) and חֹזֶה (*cho-zeh*), which are used to describe prophets who רָאָה (*ra-ah*) "see."[4] When the Bible uses this word *see* it sometimes describes seeing, beholding, becoming aware, or becoming visible, but it is also used to mean "to experience." This is important to note because, although we most commonly assume that the language and title of "seer" indicates sight and vision, these prophets may also feel, sense—even taste and smell!

> **Seers have a sense-based revelation and often a sense-based response to the revelation.**

Seers love worship and they love the emotions that come from it. Prophetic revelation goes deeply to their core, and they have a sense-based revelation and often a sense-based response to the revelation.

It is noteworthy that most people start their revelatory journey by seeing pictures. Then, after time and exercise, it becomes clearer which is your dominant receiving mode—language, sight, or emotion.

You can quickly tell which Bible prophets are seers because of the descriptive language that they use. For example, Ezekiel describes "wheels within wheels," complete with eyes, movement, sound, and with God seated on the throne outside the center of the earth. I love how God coaches Ezekiel in his seer gifting by asking him several times, "Ezekiel, what do you see?" Ezekiel replies with vivid descriptions of boiling pots and almond trees—and then God provokes a conversation to help him understand and learn the meaning of the visions. This is a massive lesson for seer prophets. They must learn to work with deep emotions and detailed sight yet be able to communicate helpfully to the rest of us as to how this might be applied on earth and what it might mean, rather than just get lost in the personal joy of an experience with God.

Isaiah's pictorial language to describe what would not happen for another 700 years (the lashing of Jesus—"by His stripes we are healed") takes us into a deep, emotional response because of the richness of the image.

Strengths of the Seer

This ability to take us on memorable, visionary journeys of revelation is such an asset of seer prophets. They provoke us with vivid descriptions and balanced emotions. Their strength lies in the power of image, feelings, and responses from God that they lean into.

Addressing the Weaknesses of Seers

On the other hand, a weakness that seers always must be alert to and working on is that they stray into territory that is too emotive—and the seer becomes too emotional—that they miss sight of what is around them and needs to be shifted here on planet Earth. Further, seers sometimes struggle for acceptance because they get bogged down in the detail of images that are of no real use to those around them. To help seers with this, I encourage them to practice by first receiving a picture but then not mentioning that picture when they prophesy. They are only allowed to use the picture as a "trigger" to bring forth the word of the Lord.

Over the years I have been fascinated to see how much the *nabi* and seer can struggle to understand each other. They are very different, and each see each other as quite peculiar—even by prophetic standards—yet when they work together there is such a fullness of expression of the incredible vastness of God!

> **When nabi and seers work together there is such a fullness of expression of the incredible vastness of God!**

THE WATCHMAN PROPHET

> *Son of man, I have made you a watchman for the people of Israel; so hear the word I speak and give them warning from me* (Ezekiel 3:17 NIV).

A common dictionary definition of *watchman* is "a person whose job it is to watch and guard a property at night or when the owners are away."[5] (In this section I am going to use the term *watchman* for brevity, but of course the role can be performed by either sex.) Bible dictionaries and lexicons give a fuller use for the word: a watchman is someone who spies or watches closely, expectantly, sometimes with a sense of stealth and subterfuge, gaining insight into enemy strategy. The first function of this sort of prophet is to warn. They usually excel in intercession, praying the bad out and the good in.

In the contemporary church we have coined the term *watchman intercessor*, which is not found in Scripture and which I don't much like. This two-word phrase assigns prayer to a specialist group and not to the entirety of the body of Christ, where it should be. I also believe that it demeans the watchmen and tends to kick them out of their prophetic office, thinking that they *only* pray rather than pray *and* prophesy, which is what they should be doing.

The watchman *is* a prophet.

The watchman concept appears thirty-six times in the Old Testament. Darris McNeely has vividly described the importance of the role in the life of the communities of the ancient Near East:

> In the ancient world of agrarian societies, large watchtowers were placed overlooking the fields. There, in the weeks the crops were ripening toward harvest, men would stand watch, guarding the fields from animals or from thieves who would make off with the crops. With the community's basic food stores at stake, the watchman's role was critical to the townspeople.
>
> We also find several references in Scripture to a watcher mounting the city walls in times of stress to survey the scene outside the fortifications. [They were] situated on a spot from which [they] could monitor the approaches to the town. If a threat

appeared, [they] would sound a warning and the town would shut its gates and prepare for battle.

You can also imagine the watcher standing vigil at other times, observing the daily life of the city. [They] could see much of the activity in the streets and markets. [They] knew the people, their work, their habits and their lifestyles.[6]

Strengths of the Watchman

Today, watchmen prophets sound alarms and deliver messages of warning. They see what has been let in in the past that is causing problems today (either by direct demonic attack or collective sin), and they often have a strong sense of urgency to make things right. Their strengths are in detailed problem sourcing, identifying roots of strongholds, and they are usually very devoted to spiritual warfare—and love houses of prayer!

> **Watchmen see the demonic and sinful roots of problems and strongholds and are usually very devoted to spiritual warfare.**

Addressing the Weaknesses of Watchmen

The weaknesses of watchmen are that they tend to be showing you a problem around every corner, and they can get bogged down in identificational repentance when it has been already long ago accomplished. This means that they can rob themselves and the people of being able to forthtell the future—seeing what

> **Watchmen should know when the glory is coming, when it is harvest time, when it is war time, and when the season is changing.**

is the coming good on the horizon. Therefore, they must learn to choose to share heavenly things as well as the demonic and be balanced with calling in the future plans of God, as much as planning prayer strikes to pull out the bad. They should know when the glory is coming, when it is harvesting time, when it is war time, and when the season is changing.

Watchmen, remember that you are prophets and so that gives you three functions: revelation, intercession, and proclamation. Often the public proclamation of the watchman is missed because the prayer room becomes too comfortable. But heed what Scripture says:

> When I say to a wicked person, "You will surely die," and you do not warn them or speak out to dissuade them from their evil ways in order to save their life, that wicked person will die for their sin, and I will hold you accountable for their blood. But if you do warn the wicked person and they do not turn from their wickedness or from their evil ways, they will die for their sin; but you will have saved yourself (Ezekiel 3:18 NIV).
>
> I have posted watchmen on your walls, Jerusalem; they will never be silent day or night (Isaiah 62:6 NIV).

You can be held to account for not prophesying and you can get oppressed because you are out of the will of God for not speaking. Silence is disobedience. Watchmen, know that the demons will always want you in a cave of muteness and hidden from being useful as a voice!

DON'T GET STUCK IN ONE WAY!

Across the spectrum of the prophets, you will find varieties of these three dominant ways of revelation. One of our prophetic errors across the whole world is to over-pigeonhole or assign a style to someone, therefore trapping that prophet from the full spectrum of how God seeks to communicate.

While each prophet tends to have a dominant and most comfortable way that they hear from God and express revelation, if they only limit themselves to this way, they will become stunted. The *nabi* must learn how to see and feel, the seer must learn how to flow with words, the watchmen must step out of the prayer room to decree the good and express the emotions of God. If you are deficient in one way, then you must give yourself to practice and learn the breadth of how God expresses Himself.

> **If you only limit yourself to one way of revelation you will become stunted.**

Prayer

Jesus, I thank You that You have called me to steward revelation. I do not want to miss all the ways You express Yourself to me.

ACTIVATION

Put your hands on your belly and ask for a flow of revelation to erupt from inside of you. Then put your hands on your heart and ask God to share His emotional status with you. Now put your hands on your eyes and ask that you might see and perceive in the spirit realm. Finally, put your hands on your feet and pray that you can take your place as a watchman standing on the wall, taking responsibility to receive the good and banish the bad.

Prayer

> *Jesus, I take responsibility to flow as a nabi, seer, and watchman prophet. I commit myself to training, and to the lifestyle that builds my revelatory muscle. Amen.*

CHAPTER 10

Understanding the Role of the Prophet

Misunderstood Prophets

The fact is that prophets are always a representation of a minority voice and are, overall, not listened to. As a prophetic person you will never speak for the majority; you will often speak what is uncomfortable; you will never win a popularity contest. If lots of people do like you, start asking questions as to whether you are doing the right thing! It is often only after what a prophet has said has come true that they are then listened to. Which leads to the misconception that prophets are all about future telling. They are not future

> **Prophets are not future or forth-telling "vending machines."**

or forth-telling "vending machines." Telling what is to come is part of it, but far from all of it.

Of course, prophets *are* human, and we generally do want to be received, understood, and do a good communication job.

However, we often don't know how to achieve this. When we do lots of future telling for people who want us to be like a spiritual horoscope, we feel used, because we are *not* only wired by God to predict people's destinies. And when we do lots of word of knowledge revelation, we feel the reward of accuracy in the moment (and it allows the people to "ooooh" and "aaahhhh" at how spot-on we might be), but it majorly drops the ball on our main role to secure the future of nations by forth-telling.

Prophets are routinely misunderstood. Even the prophets who contributed to the Bible seem easy to misconstrue, even to our wisest of theologians:

> [Reading Jeremiah for the first time gives the impression of] extreme disarray…a hopeless hodgepodge.
>
> —JON BRIGHT, Old Testament theologian[1]

> They [the prophets] have a queer way of talking, like people who, instead of proceeding in an orderly manner, ramble off from one thing to the next, so you cannot make head or tail of them or see what they are getting at.
>
> —MARTIN LUTHER, Protestant reformer[2]

The biblical prophets write for people who have processed the Torah over a lifetime, and they communicate in a cyclical, symphonic, rhythmic repetition that builds into some shape. But they are not quick to get to that point! Reading or listening to the prophets is a bit like going to an art gallery or sampling a fine wine. We ask, "How do I appreciate this picture?" or think to ourselves, "This fine wine—I'm sure it should be telling me something. I will nod and look like I understand it, but really, I'm not sure how it applies to my life, or how to interpret it."

Many prophets speak like this today: symbolism laden without clear time frames or application. Most people have no grid for hearing even a straight-talking prophet. Therefore, the revelatory community must expect to help people interpret what was said. You must expect to have to clarify; be ready for long conversations with leadership teams who *want* to understand but are just not sure how.

If thousands of commentaries are needed to help us grasp what the canonical biblical prophets are saying, how much more will you have to explain and re-explain what you felt God was saying? We might think that the word we have brought is very clear, and then get irritated, saying, "Come on—isn't it so obvious?" but rarely do people receive it as such.

> **Prophets must expect and be ready to clarify and help people interpret revelation.**

I once prophesied over someone about a capping on their lives and a controlling church situation that he had to walk away from. When I had finished prophesying, the man said to me, "Do you know, every prophet tells me the same thing!" I asked him, "Did you realize that you *actually* have to action this? Did you realize that you have to respond?" It hadn't been clear to him that any participation on his part was required. The repeated word was that he had to move on, but it hadn't been clear in his mind that prophecy was supposed to *shift* him, not just give a running commentary on his life!

Prophets, you will have to ask Jesus for the growth of the fruit of kindness so that you might be patient to explain to and support those whom you prophesy over. Remember that the anointing on you is provocative and challenging—sometimes even before you have opened your mouth! You can walk into a room, totally silently, and still annoy people because your anointing pushes them into decision making, choices, and a better status with God. So be *relationally safe*, with an irritating anointing! In other words, invest in relationships, so that you are personally trustworthy, thus making space for your anointing to bring godly challenge. Many prophets have never pursued healthy relationships with their church leadership, so when they bring a word, there is no relational track to journey that word along. But the reality is that all of us only take personal correction in our lives from trusted voices who we know love us. It is no different for the prophet challenging a church or community. The prophet must be known as one who loves and is relationally on their side.

> Be relationally safe, with an irritating anointing! The prophet must be known as one who loves and is relationally on a church leader's side.

Prophets, because you are the minority voice and you are not easily understood, and because you speak against the current of the day, take care to be clear and stay in places of giving explanation until the church gets used to working with what the prophets bring.

Prayer

I bless you in Jesus' name to learn the journey of relational safety and integrity while never having to dull your prophetic sword. Amen!

Activation

If you know that you were not relationally safe and were subsequently rejected, you will need to fix the relational basis that was not strong enough to support your prophetic words. Take time to go and heal relationships that you broke. Perhaps this is still a "live" situation? What steps can you now take to build a relationally safe connection with those whom you are called to support with your prophetic call?

PROPHETS ARE DIVINE SPOKESMEN

Prophets wrestle with questions like, "Should I prophesy the future, do I comment on the present, or do I war over history? Where do I start? Do I think past, present, or future as my default setting? Is one start point better than another?" If you asked most people, they would probably assume that "future" is the starting point. However, while future prediction is certainly something that prophets do sometimes, it is not their main biblical role.

For clarity of definition, future prediction is calling the uncreated future to form and come into being; it is *not* "fortune-telling," which is divination, but is seeing the future as God intends it to be, often pointing forward to the highest and best for a person, nation, or situation—or creating the space for God to bring correction and alignment.

We get a steer on the "how" to these questions from the life of Moses. Although Abraham is named as a prophet, it is Moses who has a divine, radical encounter with God and then sets the tone for what prophets do. Moses is the first prophet, our prototype, and it is the biography of Moses that becomes the first prophetic job description. We learn how we should be from his life. This is the conversation that God has with Moses at the burning bush:

> *Now when the Lord spoke to Moses in Egypt, he said to him, "I am the Lord. Tell Pharaoh king of Egypt everything I tell you."*
>
> *But Moses said to the Lord, "Since I speak with faltering lips, why would Pharaoh listen to me?"*
>
> *Then the Lord said to Moses, "See, I have made you like God to Pharaoh, and your brother Aaron will be your prophet. You are to say everything I command you, and your brother Aaron is to tell Pharaoh to let the Israelites go out of his country* (Exodus 6:28–7:2 NIV).

There might not be anything more shocking to read in your job description than that of Exodus 6: "*See, I have made you like God*" or, "*I will make you as God to Pharaoh*" (NASB)! You, prophet, are not just a spokesman. You are the divine voice, the divine spokesman. You are *like God* to people; you speak whatever message God wants said. One translator interprets this passage as, "I have appointed you THE GOD in this situation." You declare the mind of God—but not just the mind. You *act* with power to reinforce what God is saying. In word and action, Moses became, to Pharaoh *as* God—powerful, wonderworking, irresistible. (Let nobody foolishly misrepresent what I am writing. I am not saying that we *are* God. We are always, completely and utterly, His servants.)

PROPHETS NEED PROPHETS

We find in the life of Moses another truism: prophets need prophets. God allows for the weakness and self-distrust of Moses and gives him his own prophet. In Exodus 7:1 we read that "Aaron shall be your prophet." Aaron will serve two roles, not only prophesying but also being the interpreter of Moses' will to others, supporting Moses. The gift of Aaron as Moses' prophet is remarkable. This gift raised his courage and spirits and kept him brave and sharp.

I know how differently I minster when I have another prophet standing with me. It goes way beyond just atmospheric and revelatory agreement and takes you into a more robust emotional place. It covers insecurities, making you a purer stream, and it gives you the space to debrief, sharpen, and check that you are hearing God correctly. From this point on, Moses' diffidence, shyness, and lack of confidence completely disappears.

> You are not just a spokesman, you are a divine spokesman. In word and action you become like God to people.

Once Moses is launched upon his Heaven-directed course, certain of his miraculous powers, knowing he is as God to Pharaoh, Moses can commit to a struggle with the powerful

Egyptian king. You would never stand before powerful leaders or powerful people as a prophet in your own humanity, unless you knew you spoke for/as God, and that He would back you up. Moses, who had feared appearing a second time before Pharaoh (who was so much his worldly superior), is reminded by Aaron that *he* is, in truth, very much Pharaoh's superior. If Pharaoh has earthly power, Moses has unearthly power. He is to Pharaoh "*as a god*," with a right to command his obedience and with a strength to enforce his commands.

If the phrase, "*See, I have made you like God to Pharaoh*," doesn't have you trembling on your knees as a job description, then I don't know what else will! It will make you cry to be burned by the purifying fire of God and to give your life afresh to such an overwhelming role.

Prayer

> *Father God, dissolve the finite in me and fuse me with Your infinite thinking, so that anytime I prophesy, I might know that I speak with Your authority, and that I may do so exactly as You have intended. God, lead me in the fear of the Lord that I might fulfill my function before You. In Jesus' name, amen.*

SPEAKING AS A PROPHET

How then, therefore, should we phrase our prophetic revelation, considering what we are learning from Moses? It is understandable why prophets who are in the emerging place—who are not yet sure of their accuracy and do not have an established track record—would say things like, "I feel…" or "I think that…" but, honestly, nobody wants to know what you think you feel! You're a prophet, after all—people want to know what God thinks and feels!

Instead, many prophets default to phrases like, "I hear the Spirit of the Lord say," which is a *slight* lessening of the full prophet office, which should speak as God would in a situation.

It is preferable to announce, "I hear the Spirit of the Lord saying..." followed by the word, and then to add, "please apply biblical wisdom and test these words." When you move into prophetic commentary, you stop seeding revelation in deep places. Prophecy must be prophesied!

If you sit in front of me and I say, "*I think* God loves you," or "*I feel* God wants you to experience His love more deeply," although I might well have heard this from God, I have unfortunately couched it in language of my own opinion, and therefore, it is not pure prophecy. But if I say, "I hear the Spirit of the Lord say that He loves you," we're now stepping more toward shifting your life by revelation.

But now let's step further into our call to be a prophet. Look at the examples of Moses and other prophets in Scripture. From studying them, it seems that the most biblically accurate way to precede a prophecy would be to say, "I the Lord your God!" You are God's spokesperson, after all. If I become God's spokesperson and speak on His behalf, the example above will sound more like this: "I, your God, will encounter you with waves of My love to new levels."

Do you hear the difference? The word brings a completely different transformation to your life when it is properly prophesied. When you speak as the divine voice, God will back you up with signs and wonders. This will lead you into new understandings of the power of God that He has assigned to you.

Elijah models something similar when he becomes the divine voice:

> *Now Elijah the Tishbite, from Tishbe in Gilead, said to Ahab, "As the Lord, the God of Israel, lives, whom I serve, there will be neither dew nor rain in the next few years except at my word" [some translations have "at my command"]* (1 Kings 17:1 NIV).

He ties the weather to his own voice, telling them that unless he speaks, there will be no rain, because Elijah is acting *as God* in this situation. It is a remarkable understanding of authority and of the level of partnership that God wants with His prophets. We see the same concept at the opening of Jeremiah 2:1-2 (NIV):

> *The word of the Lord came to me: "Go and proclaim in the hearing of Jerusalem: 'This is what the Lord says: "I remember...."'"*

God asks the young prophet Jeremiah to start the prophetic word with the word "I." So when Jeremiah stood and proclaimed to Jerusalem, he would have spoken in a divine voice, as if he is God speaking.

> **Prophets must speak with authority as heralds, as official messengers of the King of Kings.**

We speak as spokespeople, or heralds of the King. Prophets are the official messengers of God, whether you or I like it or not, and whether we are comfortable with it or not!

THE PROPHET'S JOB DESCRIPTION

Ultimately the job description of the prophet is this:

You represent God, as God;

however He wants to be seen;

however He wants to sound;

and whatever He wants to say

(which is sometimes about the future).

Even the biblical prophets didn't always enjoy this main role of saying whatever the Lord wanted them to say. Jeremiah admits that he would rather not tell what God is asking of him, but God will let the revelation burn him if he won't say it (see Jeremiah 20:9). We are compelled to speak, no matter how *we* feel about it. If we will not speak, we don't just get indigestion, we get "God's word is a fire in our bones," bring-ing an internal, gnawing, silent pain. Have you ever linked your physical well-being to your silence before? When you speak you are well!

> If we will not speak, we don't just get indigestion, we get "God's word is a fire in our bones," bringing an internal, silent pain.

Over the years I have found that the greater the anointing that rests on me while I am delivering a prophetic word, the more I fear God in that moment, and man almost becomes invisible. This means that I can say whatever He needs said, whatever the cost, because my life is pledged to be His voice. Fearing God versus fearing man must be resolved in the life of the prophet, otherwise you will always be semi-impotent in your revelation. It means that, whenever I take a seat after prophesying, one of the first thoughts is, "Lord, did I represent You well, because I spoke as You—which is the job You gave me, after all?"

NATIONAL PROPHETS, SHAPING DECISIONS

The fact that Moses is the prototypical prophet has already been stated. Let's unpack this some more. Moses is purposely introduced to give us the paradigm of what a prophet is. From him onward, it is God's tradition to use prophets in how He builds the history of nations. Everyone in the Bible is a part of this prophetic tradition; they expected prophets to be present when the nation was in need. Today we are building this understanding back into the nations once again.

Moses is often seen wrangling in conversation with God on his nation's behalf, especially during their wilderness years. Similarly, Abraham is called a prophet at the point of his strident conversation with God over the number of righteous that might bring city-saving amidst the judgment against Sodom and Gomorrah. We start to see that the prophet can have a dialoguing conversation with God, not just a receiving-of-revelation relationship. The fate of the people hangs on the prophets, whom God intentionally invites into His council to help Him shape His decision making. This is the height of the prophet-calling and is as profound as it is relationally deep.

The last thing written in the Pentateuch, the five books of Moses, is this:

> *Since then, no prophet has risen in Israel like Moses, whom the Lord knew face to face, who did all those signs and wonders the Lord sent him to do in*

Egypt—to Pharaoh and to all his officials and to his whole land. For no one has ever shown the mighty power or performed the awesome deeds that Moses did in the sight of all Israel (Deuteronomy 34:10-12 NIV).

This passage offers an opportunity for prophets who have not yet ever stepped into the full Moses paradigm to arise. It is asking, "Where are the prophets like Moses?" This Scripture is provoking you to have a look for prophets like Moses. Moses is the standard of how you measure prophets.

Moses was not a one-off. In Deuteronomy, God also promises that He *"will raise up for them a prophet like you"* (Deuteronomy 18:18 NIV). Up to this point there had been an understanding that there would be a succession of priests, judges, and of kings in the Mosaic legislation. But from this verse onward, God establishes the succession of the prophets. It is the

> **The fate of the people hangs on the prophets, whom God intentionally invites into His council to help Him shape His decision making.**

verse that births generations of prophets, to its apex perfection in Christ Jesus, and even beyond, I would argue, into the present day.

It seems that God so loved His interaction and partnership with Moses, their co-laboring conversations about the nation, and having someone who spoke "as Him," that He birthed a line of *nabi* for all time.[3] The spirit and anointing of Moses is supposed to pervade the whole succession *all* prophets, including those of us who are now in Christ. While other biblical prophets might further expand our prophet job description, none was better than Moses until Jesus. If any prophet does not meet the gold standard set by Moses, it is because they lack the combination of the four key elements of his life:

1. encounters of glory

2. intense friendship with God

3. stridency of voice

4. demonstration of power that God had loved in Moses

When the prophets in Scripture are at their best, they are like Moses. Even Elijah goes back to Mount Sinai (the place of the burning bush where God's glory passed by Moses) to try to reboot the covenant with God, trying to capture what Moses had.

What the Job Requires of Us

We who are in the line of the prototype prophet Moses, we who are birthed as his seed, we who are created with his anointing, we who share the same Spirit of Yahweh—we are being asked to come up to the level of Moses! What does this require? It requires that you go to sleep as a prophet, you wake up as a prophet, you eat as a prophet. It never switches off; it is who you are. It requires a level of obedience, flexibility, and

> God may let you have your preferences, but He will not let you keep your prejudices.

moldability that most won't ever attain. God may let you have your preferences (favorite color, fashion, and food, for example), but He will not let you keep your prejudices. It requires strength and determination to speak as an imperfect human, channeling the voice of the Perfect.

I often think that it is a very odd thing that God asks us to do this at all. He knows our sin, our frailty, our humanity, and yet He asks us to bring forth perfected words. This is why we should continually be asking God things like, "Did I say that the way You wanted it, Lord?" "Did I represent You rightly?" and, "Was my tone, Your tone?" The joy (and perhaps relief!) for those of us prophesying today is that the New Testament guards us with instructions for the rest of the body of believers to weigh prophecy (see 1 Corinthians 14:29). The New Covenant gracefully covers us by explaining to everyone that we only know in part and prophesy in part (see 1 Corinthians 13:9), and by giving instruction to the church to test and not be deceived by wrong spirits (see 1 John 4:1).

WHEN YOU GET IT WRONG

Let's be real. Most of us are unlikely to find ourselves in the same territory as Samuel, with not a word falling to the ground. Therefore, to keep the absolute integrity of the prophetic movement intact, it is vital that prophets repent when they miss it. You unequivocally bring the prophetic into complete disrepute when you will not repent for error. It is not wisdom to hide behind the calendar using, "Well, one day it will happen" excuses. If you gave a measurably timed word and it plainly turns out to be wrong, fix it. Please see that the body of Christ so needs prophets that we must have—and operate in—a higher level of personal integrity.

We should be glad of the opportunity to repair and put things right! Simply repent and explain that we see in part and that we do our best.

The Old Covenant punishment for people who prophesied things that were not from God is death. We are under a better covenant now, but even still, I have personally witnessed prophets be retired, lose everything, lose their minds, or even die suddenly when they have been walking out of step with the call of God. If you are going to say "yes" to this most serious of vocations, please remain humble and quick to repent. Your life on this earth may even depend on it!

I think it is fascinating that according to Scripture only Samuel is recorded as having 100 percent accuracy with his words. This could suggest that the other Bible prophets were not always spot on! Now, let me be super-clear, the Bible is our completely reliable, God-breathed authority and we can totally, utterly rely on the words of the prophets that we have been given and are recorded in it. But perhaps, outside of the canon of Scripture, we might assume that that they were not always totally, 100 percent "on it," because only Samuel has this accolade (as far as we are told). No prophet was a perfect, sinless, infallible human after all—save for Jesus. Maybe they all had their "Jonah moments."

> You unequivocally bring the prophetic into complete disrepute when you will not repent for error.

Leaders, what would you do in a modern-day prophet's shoes; how would you make a decision regarding the revelation that you allow in your church? Would you want prophets to silence the voice of God just in case their humanity leaks out a little bit? Or would you want them to partner with boldness and fulfill the function that they have been given in the body of Christ—even if the vessel is frail?

Before prophesying in a church, it can be helpful to have a conversation with the leaders that involves asking them some questions about the level of responsibility that they are willing to take over what you are going to say. I might ask them, "Do you want me to stop prophesying in your church, because you must know that I will always be human and so might occasionally misstep? In doing so you will deprive the church of the prophetic voice of God. Or are you prepared to work with the New Testament over what is prophesied: weigh and test, and take *your* responsibility with the words?"

> Would you want prophets to silence the voice of God in your church, just in case their humanity leaks out? But prophets must always be prepared to acknowledge when they miss it.

All of this is a further reminder of why prophets must always be prepared to acknowledge when they miss it. Certainly, as maturity in revelation develops, I expect and generally find that the accuracy, reliability, and trustworthiness of a prophet's word improves.

Some Top Tips for Emerging Prophets

1. Hold Your Words Lightly

Over the years, I have had different members of my prophetic team come to me after they have ministered and say things like, "We can't work with that group again. They ignored our prophetic words."

But that attitude does not sit well with me, and I have had to correct my team: it is *not* our responsibility to make the word be actioned. Once spoken, step back. Don't be too protective about your words. Hold them lightly once they are spoken, and don't let your fear or ego wrongly guard them. Let them be tested and approved.

2. You Are Rarely Responsible for Actioning the Word

Just because you see something or say something does not mean you are the one to work out the words. Therefore, once we have prophesied there is a need to ask, "How responsible am I for making this word come to pass?"

We often prophesy about people who are moving into a new house, or changing location, or shifting churches. Does that mean that because we said it, we must therefore become their removal team? No, of course not! Be sure that you know clearly what is to be prophesied and what is to become an action.

Activation

As you consider this advice, why not take a moment to ask God, "Is there anything that I am currently touching that I wasn't supposed to?" Perhaps it was supposed to be a declaration of the heart of God but not something that you were supposed to end up building. It can be easy for prophets to fall into the trap of prophesying a gap, not seeing anyone fill that gap, and then subsequently trying to pick up the tools to do it themselves. This is a surefire way to end up burnt out and exhausted.

3. Check Your Tone

Find the balance between not watering down your words for perceived acceptability, but not over-stating them for effect. On occasion the prophet's whisper is a roar. Always check with God for the right tone of delivery that you are to use.

4. Be Brave—Controversial Is OK

Be brave and speak what God gives you as a divine spokesperson. If you don't, you will dishonor your call. False prophets will always tell you what you want to hear. But our key distinctive as prophets of Yahweh is that we challenge people's sensitivities. It is why we prophets are often accused of being controversial.

We also know that when a prophet does *not* speak or is not heard, destruction comes to the people (see Proverbs 29:18). When 2 Chronicles 20:20 says, "Believe the prophets and you will prosper," it is not actually a verse about ensuring that people are blessed or financially prosperous (as is intimidatingly quoted in some churches today—that's manipulation). It means, "Listen to the prophets to make sure that you are not destroyed!" The passage in 2 Chronicles comes from the eve of a great battle against a vast enemy army. The people of Judah literally must believe the prophets to avoid being wiped out! Therefore, we don't hold back our sound because, if we do, the people don't do well.

5. *Be an Emotionally Well Prophet*

Do not ever prophesy when you know you aren't in a good place or you have an agenda! Those of us who preach and teach know that we can lecture at length from the pulpit or platform about how one builds a personally good relationship with God, but then not do it ourselves. We can literally avoid practicing what we preach! Keeping yourself emotionally well in order to steward the divine is always a challenge. Therefore, one of your regular prayers must be something along the lines of, "Lord, would You help me to not be emotionally sloppy!"

Activation

Let's face it, we are all "emotionally sloppy" on occasions, aren't we? Considering this, here are four simple, yet exceptionally effective things that you have to be quick to do and say. (I teach these to my children as much as I do to my emerging prophets whom I am raising up.) Always be fast at saying:

- I am sorry.
- I forgive you.
- Thank you.
- I love you.

6. *You Can Be Your Own Worst Prophet!*

You can be your own worst prophet, hearing things and not testing them like you would if someone else had said it. We tend to think that just because we heard the voice of God for ourselves it must be right, but we don't stop to test it by the same standards of exacting scrutiny that we place on others when they prophesy to us. Then we feel aggrieved when things don't go well. So don't be your own worst prophet! When you can learn to weigh and test your *own* revelation for yourself, then you will be much better equipped to test the revelation that you are given for those outside of yourself, and even for cities and nations.

Radical Experiences

Moses, our prototype prophet, begins his journey with a radical God-encounter at the burning bush that sets the tone for the rest of his life. He continues to go on having incredible, divine encounters over the coming decades, such as on Mount Sinai, where the glory of God passes by him, and alone at the Tent of Meeting.

Moses, the one from whom we get the basic prophetic job description, shows us that we *must* have radical experiences of God's presence so that He can bring us to a place where we simply cannot back out of the call. Therefore, if you struggle with your call in an ongoing way, the medicine is to ask the Lord for more encounters with Him.

God successfully speaking through people is linked to their encounters with God. Take the prophet Micah, for example, who writes, *"But as for me, I am filled with power, with the Spirit of the Lord, and with justice and might"* (Micah 3:8 NIV). This verse comes right in the middle of a chapter in which Micah is outing the false prophets—they proclaim "peace" if they have something to eat but prepare to wage war against anyone who refuses to feed them. In other words, they only go where the money is! That is a biblical definition of false prophet.

How is Micah different from them? How can only he say, "But as for me"? It is because he alone had an encounter that filled him with power, with the Spirit of the Lord Himself, and with justice and might. That encounter gives him the ability to remain as a true voice of the divine.

Prophets like Isaiah, Jeremiah, Amos, Habakkuk, and John the Revelator all talk about their experiences encountering God. These are not regular encounters; they write of them as frightening—they really think that they are going to die. (Many of the prophets read as if they were unhappy people who would rather not speak—if that is you, you are in good company!) But the level of encounter makes them intense people who *cannot* be quiet. When they encountered God, it was the catalyst that caused them to make a huge impact on their national history.

So as we conclude and return to the thrust of this chapter, we ask again, "What does a prophet do?" A prophet lives a lifestyle of radical, divine encounters.

God has chosen prophets to represent Him through all of human history and to reveal Him. Even in their frail, fallible, human form, they are the divine voice who know Him—perhaps better than they even know the people they are called to speak to.

Prayer

> *Lord, I embrace the revelation that I am the seed of Moses. Jesus, would You reconnect me with the anointing of Moses and graft me back into the line of prophets that I have walked away from? Jesus, would You lead me in the four things that Moses knew:*
>
> - *Encounters of glory*
> - *Intense friendship with You*
> - *Stridency of voice*
> - *Demonstrations of power*

Father God, my desire is to represent You as You want to be seen in the earth today, communicating exactly as You wish. Take my life! I rededicate it to this purpose of stewarding and becoming Your voice. In Jesus' name, amen.

SECTION TWO

THE DEEPER DIVE

*I am not afraid of storms for I am
learning how to sail my ship.*
—Amy March, from *Little
Women*, Louisa May Alcott

CHAPTER 11

PROPHESYING INTO STRUCTURES AND SYSTEMS

IF YOU WANT to create pain, if you want to maximize heartache, and if you want wounding and rejection to abound, you build a system that satan can infiltrate. You build opposite to God and His instructions. This includes getting loose and wrongly flexible with some of God's non-negotiables. You don't build a Kingdom of God structure. You don't set a biblical framework. You pray more about your organization and your nation than you do for the descending Kingdom of God to be seen in the midst of you and in its associated structures.

> If you want wounding and rejection to abound, you build a system that satan can infiltrate.

THE EARTH BELONGS TO GOD BUT SATAN RULES THE COSMOS

When satan was kicked out of heaven, he was thrown down to earth.

Then war broke out in heaven. Michael and his angels fought against the dragon, and the dragon and his angels fought back. But he was not strong enough, and they lost their place in heaven. The great dragon was hurled down—that ancient serpent called the devil, or Satan, who leads the whole world astray. He was hurled to the earth, and his angels with him. Then I heard a loud voice in heaven say: "Now have come the salvation and the power and the kingdom of our God, and the authority of his Messiah. For the accuser of our brothers and sisters, who accuses them before our God day and night, has been hurled down. They triumphed over him by the blood of the Lamb and by the word of their testimony; they did not love their lives so much as to shrink from death" (Revelation 12:7-11 NIV).

This earth was not supposed to be satan's home. He originally roamed the heavenlies, accusing us before God, day and night. But he has been thrown down to mankind's domain and we—the people of the Lamb—are now supposed to torment *him*, not the other way around! He (currently) has nowhere else to go, apart from the realm of this planet. And so, part of his miserable existence is that we crush him under our feet and build contrary to his systems!

The Bible is clear that Yahweh, our Almighty God, owns *everything*. Psalm 24 (NIV) opens with *"The earth is the Lord's, and everything in it, the world, and all who live in it."* The Hebrew word for "the earth" is אֶרֶץ *eres*, and it literally means that everything created is God's: the soils, stones, dust, regions and territories (non-political), the people, the land of the living, the foundations—it all belongs to Him.

How then, you might ask, in light of God's ownership do we deal with the verse that says that satan is the "prince of the power of the air"?[1]

> *As for you, you were dead in your transgressions and sins, in which you used to live when you followed the ways of this world and of the ruler of the kingdom of the air* [the lower air we breathe], *the spirit who is now at work in those who are disobedient* (Ephesians 2:1-2 NIV).

In this verse, Paul seems to be describing satan as the ruler of this world, our atmosphere. So what is satan actually ruling? The New Testament Greek word for "world" here is κόσμος, *kosmos*. "Cosmos," a term we still use and understand today, refers to all of the created world, especially the human systems and governments of the world that have been established. Satan rules in these, but he does not have ownership or possession.

> **Satan rules the cosmos, but he does not have ownership or possession of it.**

He has influence and rulership over "the ways of the cosmos"—human structures, human governments, and human systems. Satan has specific rulership over anything man-made and sourced in man instead of God, which is why God and Samuel are so dismayed when the elders of Israel declare that they want a *"king to lead us, such as all the other nations have"* (1 Samuel 8:5 NIV). Not only is this a rejection of the Lord as King, but to take a human king, or a monarchy, is ultimately embracing a man-made system of governing. God is pro-theocracy, where He alone rules as King in the hearts of men, delegating the operational structures and governmental processes into the earth.

GODLY STRUCTURES AND SYSTEMS

All of this should make us prophets cry out, "I want a godly structure; I want a God-made system; I want a governmental organization that is straight from heaven!" If you don't have God's structure you cannot have honor and freedom. If you don't have a God-system and instead you follow the "ways of the cosmos," satan has full liberty to infiltrate it—and that, unfortunately, means pain.

As I wrote in Chapters 4 and 5, if you have a church that does not mirror a biblical, fivefold structure, you probably have a man-made system, and therefore you have opened a door to potential satanic infiltration and horrible heartache. I wish it could be said in a more muted way, but we have set ourselves up for pain in our current church structure. Some of the churches we attend may well have begun under divine instruction, but, over time, they can become inflexible. Almost all Christian organizations have some significant form of demonic infiltration because we put in systems, courses, buildings, and structures that either were man-made or that, over time, became idols.

The enemy invites you onto his turf to play with his way of doing things, and when you step into his patch, you have given the invitation for him to have a foothold. Once he has a foothold, he will build a stronghold around it and you, and you are in a prison that you do not even realize has been constructed about you. We must therefore take up an alert, offensive position against anything that is man-made or has not been flexible enough to keep up with how the Lord would want things to be done in the here and now.

God is currently releasing prophetic iconoclasts and provokers who will help smash the vehicles that are taking us down wrong roads and who will map us back to the vision and values of the Kingdom of Jesus Christ. May I put it to you that the so-called decline of the denominational church and the emergence of new church forms is not the crisis that we think it is! And that, overall, what God is doing with the church is not leaving her to die alone but is lovingly changing her so that she might have the impact she was meant to have in hearts and minds—and not just the impact of an institutional monolith that scares people into moral submission.

> God is currently releasing prophetic iconoclasts and provokers to help us get back to the vision and values of the Kingdom.

Contrary to what we might conclude from well-researched figures showing that many of our Christian denominations and institutions are losing numbers at a rapid rate, I believe that the church is not in decline but is in a godly reformation and transformation process. Perhaps satan is not killing the church, as doomsday predictors might claim, but rather, God is letting some old and tired institutions decline, so the people of God can be more like church as He intended. *The institution of "church" may be powerless and painful, but the real church is not.*

This is not fervent anti-institutionalism, nor is this a rant against structure and organization. This is about deeply loving—and being committed to grow—a church that is power filled, presence centered, biblically pain-free, and excellently organized.

Who among us wants to keep propping up something that doesn't work—where all we do is perpetuate our pain and keep reinforcing a wrong thinking? But we do need to break, dig, and till a new ground, to create a new atmosphere that grows what Jesus intended.

THE HALDANE BROTHERS: PROVOCATIVE EXAMPLES

Fundamentally, the man-made structures that we have built and continue to prop up in the 21st century do not have (or no longer carry) the capacity to empower people, and therefore God can no longer bless them. However, we are not in a unique moment of history. The church has been here before. This is not the first time that structure, methodology, and traditions have had to be radically challenged by prophets and apostles.

Scotland in the middle of the 18th century was a very religiously uniform place. Nearly all believers were part of one denomination, the Church of Scotland ("the Kirk").[2] By the mid-to-late 1700s, the only theology seminary in Scotland taught ministers how to be good and moral people. The clergy were lectured in middle-class pursuits like hunting, shooting, and fishing, but with no real salvation message or robust, biblical training. Robert and James Haldane, brothers from the Scottish city of Dundee, were so outraged by this that they sold their considerable land inheritance to start to preach the gospel, build churches ("tabernacles") to hold the new converts, and, importantly, started five theological colleges where evangelical ministers could be trained properly.

Despite much persecution (a law was even passed to ban their newly trained ministers from preaching), within ten years this church-planting move of the Haldanes had become such a successful provocation that the Church of Scotland saw the error of its ways and began to change and copy what the Haldanes had been doing—teaching and preaching the gospel. The brothers' Bible colleges trained 300 clergy, but when the established Kirk really grasped hold of truth and started to put *their* house in order, James and Robert closed all of theirs—job done. Their work of provocation had been a success. As well as enduring incredible opposition, it is estimated that the Haldanes spent £70,000 of their own money to do this, which would be something like £10.5 million today (over $13 million). Revival historian Michael Marcel describes their impact as no less than "changing the face of Scotland." It is largely because of what they did to reset the system and raise up uncompromising, evangelical clergy that Scotland once again became known as the great missionary-sending, "Land of the Book" in the 19th century. The pioneering Haldanes had to be happy to risk rejection and be willing to be a provocation in order to change the established system.[3]

> The pioneering Haldanes had to be happy to risk rejection and be willing to be a provocation in order to change the established system.

God has a structure; in fact, He has a whole Kingdom! You are not just waiting for the return of Jesus Christ; you are waiting for a descending holy city, complete with government, structure, values, and a God-ordained culture.

A Prophecy to the Iconoclasts

Jesus says to us today:

> You have prayed that My Kingdom would come and My will would be done. Now I am going to refresh you, strengthen you, and reestablish within you My values and culture. I will sensitize you to what is of My Kingdom and what is not. I will take hold of your hand and back you as you tear down the man-made and build up and establish My Kingdom. I am with the iconoclasts.

It is vital that we don't simply flee from all structure where it has become corrupt. We must build the new, together. We don't get to run off on our own! Instead, we get our building hard hats on and form apostolic and prophetic building teams. The Lord wants us to have a God-made system, built on the foundations of the apostles and prophets, with Christ Jesus as the Chief Cornerstone. In this day we get to *architect hope* and reconnect with what Jesus meant by "church."

Right now, the Lord is releasing "building mantles" on your shoulders and gifting you with an anointing that will break the hold of tradition and that has the genius of God in it, to construct what now needs to be seen in the earth. *Prophets, if we want wholeness and wellness, this is how it starts!*

CHAPTER 12

THE MINDSET AND COMMUNITY OF A THRIVING PROPHET

IT'S A LIMITLESS KINGDOM!

As we tear down and build up, there is a set of key understandings and default mindsets that prophets must have to stay robust and whole, in shape, in a state of eudaimonia,[1] and functioning well in their call. I like to call this having a "thriving mindset."

Chief among the thoughts that lead to a mindset of thriving is that the Kingdom of God is a *limitless* Kingdom! When I have conversations with small-minded, jealous people, I will come off the phone and shout loudly in frustration, "*Don't you know that it's a limitless Kingdom!*" In the Kingdom of God there are oceans of love to get submerged in; there is mercy and forgiveness that you will never be able to find the end of; there is an eternal Father who, with undiluted, untamable, wild passion, never stops chasing you. There is kindness without pollution that never deals with you as you deserve—so you always get God on a good day. There is no ceiling. There are no limited resources. The Kingdom of

God is not a cramped place; it's a spacious place. The Kingdom is like the sky that is so big no two birds will ever collide. The Kingdom of God is not frugal; it is not moderate; it has abundance and thriving for all.

When I win and get somewhere in life, the doorway is *so* wide and the land *so* broad, others can come through as well. This means that the better my team prophesies and the better they lead, the better it is for us all. In a limitless Kingdom I have no need to be jealous, or to undermine them, or to cap them. I use my personal authority to build others to exceed me, to stand on my shoulders, and to go further than me. I should not be raising up those around me to *succeed* me (which means that I always must strive to be "higher" or "ahead of them," which leads to the burnout of me, or the crushing of them), I am building them to *exceed* me. Therefore, I do not have a succession plan, I have an expansion plan.

You need to get hold of this truth, and then shadow it into every atmosphere that you encounter. Prophets, we must lead the way in breaking agreement with one-upmanship, petty jealousies, and control. This understanding alone will medicate your heart against envy and spite. When someone does better than you, celebrate—because they have opened up a way for you to do brilliantly too! They have pressed forward into a new place that neither of you were at before.

My husband David and I have adopted an "Eighteen Month Rule." This means that around every year and a half, whatever our hands are touching we pass it on, and somebody else takes responsibility for it. The aim is that everyone around us, including ourselves, is stepping up and entering continual growth, glory to glory, and pushing deeper into the concept of the limitless Kingdom of God.

For example, in 2010 we launched "Lion Bites," our ministry's daily, free written prophetic words that we send out by email and social media to tens of thousands every day. In the early days, we took full responsibility for these; it was our baby—we wrote, edited, and sent them out. However, for many years now, these have been completely the responsibility of others within the ministry. Despite it being one of our most high-profile projects, my team is trusted to write them, edit, train and recruit the team, and develop the brand as they see fit. I do not touch them at all.

Similarly, no longer than a year after leading our Sunday gathering, Power Church, out of lockdown, it was time for me to lay hands on and bless Katrina to lead, even as the church grew, and its online influence was rocketing.

This concept of giving away always means a lot of change, and there are certainly moments when this is very tough, especially when you have become a "specialist" at something and now you must become an amateur in a new thing again! But honestly, it *mostly* works. (On occasions people do step into things beyond their competency, and we must clean up a mess. But that is OK! It's so much better than the alternative, where everyone stays stuck and limited.) Overall, the limitless Kingdom mentality will keep you with an ability to open up opportunities for all to move

> Don't build those around to succeed you, build them to exceed you. Don't have a succession plan, have an expansion plan.

up and forward, and we find great favor from God when trying to walk this out.

However, the limitless Kingdom of God will be completely contained, to dangerous levels, if the senior leader is the jealous type or insecure. People will get hope-filled that they are going to soar, but leadership insecurity will stop them. Therefore, we must tattoo this verse on the inside of our eyelids:

> **The Kingdom of God is a limitless Kingdom! There is no ceiling or limit.**

So from now on we regard no one from a worldly point of view (2 Corinthians 5:16 NIV).

It is imperative that we continually see people according to the stature that God sees them. If you *won't* do this, it will be almost impossible to see limitless blessing in your midst.

Prayer

Lay hands on your head and ask Jesus to give you a "limitless Kingdom of God" mindset. Pray:

> *Jesus, would You show me how to pull other people into the limitless way that You think, where Your love, grace, resources, and possibilities are without end. Jesus, I am sorry for any jealousy or controlling notions within me. I repent of any partnership with these things and ask that You would remove them from my life. Amen.*

YOUR PROPHETIC COMPANY
WILL ENSURE YOU THRIVE

If you really want to blossom and thrive as an emerging prophet, you will need what I call "a community of thriving." This is inspired by what Paul writes to the church in Ephesus:

> *Consequently, you are no longer foreigners and strangers, but fellow citizens with God's people and also members of his household, built on the foundation of the apostles and prophets, with Christ Jesus himself as the chief cornerstone. In him the whole building is joined together and rises to become a holy temple in the Lord. And in him you too are being built together to become a dwelling* [habitation] *in which God lives by his Spirit* (Ephesians 2:19-22, emphasis added).

There are not many habitations of the Spirit, just one. One dwelling. According to this Scripture it is not merely, "I am filled with the Spirit," it is, "*We* are filled with the Spirit." God's Spirit lives in us together. Together we are the fixed abode of God. It is not an appropriate prayer to ask, "God, make me Your address." Rather it should be, "God make *us* Your address!" There is something new that God wants to do in terms of the weight of His glory being poured out, but it comes in relational authenticity, in which we are the "living stones" built together as a place where God dwells (see 1 Peter 2:5).

I believe that one of the next battles of the church will be with our intimacy issues, our independent spirits, and our lack of vulnerability. We will have to learn or re-learn how to trust and have someone in our armpit, holding us up through the twists and turns of life.

One of the Bible stories that is dearest to my heart in terms of how we think about our base here in Glasgow is found in Acts 4. Peter and John had been arrested and thrown in jail. They were then dragged in front of the religious court, where they were hated, oppressed, and given repeated stern warnings not speak about Jesus again. All of this they refused to do and so they were sent packing, with threats of severe punishment ringing in their ears. Luke then reports that, *"On their release, Peter and John went back to their own people"* (Acts 4:23 NIV; the KJV translated this as *"their own company"*). In the hard times the apostles go to their own company, and what happens? Do they get told off for lacking wisdom? Do they get reprimanded and judged for not behaving more discreetly? Do they get told to go and take a rest break because they must have had a hard time? No! Their company raised their voices in one accord and prayed, *"Now, Lord, consider their threats and enable your servants to speak your word with great boldness. Stretch out your hand to heal and perform signs and wonders through the name of your holy servant Jesus"* (Acts 4:29-30 NIV). To paraphrase, they cried out as one, "Oh God, it's been bad—but we want more miracles!

> Your own company is the place that sees your call, understands its validity and vitalness, underpins you, and raises your arms in the tough times.

Oh God, it's been dreadful—but we want more boldness! Oh

God, we have been very hurt—but we are pushing through, together, for signs and wonders!"

Your own company, your own people, is the place that sees your call, understands its validity and vitalness, underpins you, and raises your arms in the tough times. For the prophet, who will always wrestle with the sharpness of their sword and the cuts it can make, life is almost un-survivable if you do not have these people around you. This kind of community of thriving requires deliberate, targeted, and specific investment of your time in relationships. These are the people who will encourage you by saying, "Don't let your sword become dull; keep bringing weighty revelation!"

These people are imperative when your life has been turned upside down. Your company, your tribe—those who understand the anointing and the call on your life—does not let you sit in the doldrums and speak the nonsense of Job's friends. No! They embrace the pain of the moment together with you. They press forward with you, as one.

> *After they prayed, the place where they were meeting was shaken. And they were all filled with the Holy Spirit and spoke the word of God boldly* (Acts 4:31 NIV).

Back in Acts 4, with Peter and John, God could not help but move in response to the team understanding. It opened space for a commanded blessing that was so powerful that it shook the building and brought with it a new anointing for miracles. What was the catalyst for the power of God to move? *They were with their own company!*

When Jesus rose from the grave, He preached to the 500, but by the time of the Upper Room experience, there were only

120 left! I surmise that those who left just couldn't stomach the togetherness, intense belonging, and the push for more, even in opposition. All of Heaven waited until there was a unity of hearts; all of Heaven must have watched with bated breath until they were completely of one accord. What was the catalyst for the power of God to move? What provoked Heaven to move? Not numbers, but one heart, one accord, one place.

Prayer

Most of us don't instinctively find ourselves amid our own company, especially not as prophetic people. So let's pray:

> Jesus, I ask in Your name that You would help me gather and lead a tribe of revelators who will keep each other's swords sharp, understand each other's call, and push into the fullness of miracles, signs, and wonders. Amen!

YOUR PROPHETIC COMPANY WILL ENSURE YOUR PROPHECIES COME TO PASS

In chapters 8 to 10 of 1 Samuel, we read the story of the anointing of Saul as the first king of Israel. When we first meet Saul, he is out looking for his father's lost donkeys. After searching far and wide for some time, Saul still can't find the missing animals and so he seeks the help of the prophet Samuel, who he hopes will be able tell him where they are. After all, he has been told that with Samuel, everything he says comes true.

Now, I've never been asked to source missing donkeys before, but I have been asked many times about errant cats! One time, a lady approached me, wanting to know where her elderly cat had run away to. When I asked her how long her cat had been missing, she replied, "Twenty years." When I answered her with, "Unfortunately I think that cat is dead," she asked if that was a word from God. "No, cats don't live that long," was my reply!

Back to 1 Samuel: Saul meets Samuel in the gateway of a town but doesn't yet realize that he is face to face with the great prophet himself. Samuel is not caught off guard, however, because God had spoken to him the day before, revealing that the next day he will meet the man who he is to anoint as king. Saul is literally head and shoulders above his peers. Physically he is handsome, an impressive young man without equal among the Israelites. His father, Kish, was a man of standing, a valiant warrior, powerful, and influential.

Saul sees none of this greatness himself and seems to have self-esteem issues. When Samuel tells him that, "You are the desire of Israel, the one we are waiting on," Saul replies, "But…I am from the smallest tribe…my family is the least of the families. I have no idea why you are talking to me like this about such great things." There is a wall between Saul and his greatness, and he doesn't think anyone should be waiting on someone as insignificant as him. May I suggest that this is a man who doesn't know how loved he is and therefore cannot accept the greatness that is assigned to him because he has not had those around him who reinforce who he truly is. Saul compares himself to his parents' greatness, and in doing so reduces himself, because comparison erodes your ability to be great.

Subsequently, Samuel, as he discharges Saul, prophesies that he will meet a company of prophets, will prophesy with them, and will be changed into a different person. That is exactly what happened! Saul does meet a tribe of prophets and is transformed into becoming another man—actually, he is changed back into the person he was supposed to be. He comes into remembrance of his call.

What we learn from this story is that you can *have* a prophetic word over your life, but it takes a prophetic culture to *cultivate* the word. It takes a prophetic culture around you to help you become the person God said you were to be. Some words don't come to pass because you are not with people who understand prophecy and the greatness of God that is within you. Without these people to surround you with Heaven's truth, the words don't come to life, and you cannot metamorphosize into who you are called to be. Your own company is indispensable for the full activation of the revelation that is spoken into your life. You should yearn for days with prophets, because being with your own company of prophets will make you feel more alive than at any other time. You shadow each other into illustriousness! Isolation doesn't deal with blind spots, but in togetherness iron sharpens iron.

You must beware the Obadiah spirit as you make your journey of emerging as a prophet. Obadiah was a righteous man in the days of Elijah who accidently divided the prophets. Wicked Queen Jezebel was on the warpath, looking for prophets' blood, and so Obadiah hid all the prophets in two caves. In doing so he invertedly separated them and broke the agreement and courage that they collectively carried. Poor Elijah was left thinking that he was the only one left. Beware righteous people who are seeking to divide the prophets, because when the prophets are not

> You can have a prophetic word over your life, but it takes a prophetic culture to cultivate the word.

in relationship with each other and are in separate camps, it makes a space for Jezebel. Prophets then mistakenly believe that they are alone—and, as a result, they are radically diminished in their function.

The level of proximity that a tribe or company produces can be an overwhelming thought for many of us. Within the atmosphere of revelation, where the spirit of prophecy hovers and is warmly invited in, there aren't many secrets! There is a journey into knowing and being known that at the doorway requires you to deal with any offend-ability in your heart.

Your Prophetic Company Will Sharpen You

I grew up in Northern Ireland and, although I've now spent more time out of her than living in her, the culture that shaped me most was the Irish one. It is real, authentic, bold, uncompromising, stubborn, and direct. Often my heart yearns for the Northern Irish black sense of humor and the straight-talking, no-nonsense approach to conversations. Perhaps a nation that has seen civil war, bombs, and much death within living memory doesn't need to dress itself up.

In Northern Ireland you can say to your friend, "That lipstick color looks awful on you," and they will smile and thank you for letting them know. You will often hear the sharpening question, "Who reared you?" (meaning "who raised you—who brought you up?") when you do something silly, as a way of publicly being told that you need to stop that behavior. The bluntness of the culture sometimes surprises the onlooker, and it may even be considered rude to those not familiar with the Northern Irish way. How many of us are in full embrace of Proverbs 27:5-6?

Open rebuke is better than love carefully concealed.
Faithful are the wounds of a friend (NKJV).

Better is open rebuke than hidden love. Wounds from
a friend can be trusted (NIV).

A truly good friend will openly correct you. You can
trust a friend who corrects you (CEV).

Do you have an unoffendable heart, one that allows friends to get alongside you and speak truth? Or do you flee from all criticism and shaping? I am increasingly hearing the error taught that prophetic words should bring harmony rather than challenge. This false teaching is appearing because in our hearts we prefer independence, our version of the truth, and a say-nothing culture that does not raise challenges to who we are and how we choose to behave. Challenging our friends (or allowing them to challenge us) is increasingly not our way. Yet doesn't Paul tell us to speak the truth in love (see Ephesians 4:15)?

> We need people in our lives who love us but who are not afraid to speak hard truths to us with "loving teeth."

We all need people in our lives who love us but who are not afraid to speak hard truths to us when necessary—I call this having "loving teeth." Are we brave enough to cry out, "Come into my life, friends who have 'loving teeth,' and please don't leave me as you find me! Come friends, into my life, and tell me courageously who I am meant to be! Come friends, into my life, and sharpen me into the image of Christ! Come friends, into my life, because I have chosen un-offendability. Come friends, into my life, and faithfully trim away my rough edges!"

YOUR PROPHETIC COMPANY WILL REPEL YOUR ENEMIES

One final thought about the amazing benefits of being with a prophetic company: by the time you have mastered the full blessing of iron-sharpening-iron, not only will your tribe enable your prophetic words to come to pass, but they will also repel the enemy on your behalf. Let's move to a much later story in the life of Saul. By chapter 19 of 1 Samuel, Saul is fully established and reigning as king, but a young shepherd-boy-turned-giant-slayer, David, has been anointed by Samuel to be the next monarch. Saul, who has fallen back into his old insecurities, is insanely jealous of the popular king-to-be and spends years trying to track him down across Israel. We come to a particular tale of Saul attempting to capture David, which becomes almost comical when the weight of the spirit of prophecy wreaks havoc in the lives of the men sent to arrest him:

> *Word came to Saul: "David is in Naioth at Ramah";*
> *so he sent men to capture him. But when they saw a*
> *group of prophets prophesying, with Samuel standing*
> *there as their leader, the Spirit of God came on Saul's*
> *men, and they also prophesied. Saul was told about*
> *it, and he sent more men, and they prophesied too.*
> *Saul sent men a third time, and they also prophesied.*
> *Finally, he himself left for Ramah and went to the*
> *great cistern at Seku. And he asked, "Where are*
> *Samuel and David?"*

"Over in Naioth at Ramah," they said.

So Saul went to Naioth at Ramah. But the Spirit of God came even on him, and he walked along prophesying until he came to Naioth. He stripped off his garments, and he too prophesied in Samuel's presence. He lay naked all that day and all that night. This is why people say, "Is Saul also among the prophets?" (1 Samuel 19:19-24 NIV)

The anointing of a prophetic company will repel the enemy, even when that enemy has murderous thoughts about you.

Prayer

Jesus, we love what You did in the days of Saul, David, and Samuel. Would you renew this in our day and time? Oh Jesus, send Your Spirit of revelation once again to Your people, that it might shadow them and even those who seek to do us harm! Jesus, we cry out that You would graft us into our own company. Open and lead us in the way of the unoffendable. In Jesus' name, amen.

We will return to this topic and consider what modern prophetic companies look like in the penultimate chapter of this book.

CHAPTER 13

DEALING WITH WOUNDING

DEALING WITH PROPHET-STUCK-IN-WOUNDING is one of the major Achilles' heels of the prophetic community. You may be able to cover your wounding for years, but eventually it will leak out on your platform.

WOUNDED PROPHETS ARE DANGEROUS PROPHETS

Most of a prophet's wounding will stem from rejection; the prophet carrying rejection is a dangerous prophet. Rejection will flavor our prophecy and will contaminate revelation. It opens the door for accidental demonic partnership, in which demons will target hurts and wounds, and unfortunately, many prophets—perhaps more than most people in general—have an undealt-with root of rejection. It may be that you were different, or you stood out, even from as far back as your childhood years. It may be that now the local church

> Rejection comes through many channels, and it is poison for the prophet.

doesn't understand your gift and has rejected you, along with God's voice. Rejection comes through many channels, and it is poison for the prophet because it opens the door to control, fear of man, fear of failure, and a host of other ungodly emotions.

We must get free from rejection and the fear of man, continually examining our hearts for traces of this disease, so we don't find ourselves in the company of false prophets. Woundedness usually manifests in defensiveness and aggression (the desire to always be right, which means that it is hard for you to have anyone test your prophetic words without you overreacting). It also can be a breeding ground for an "empire spirit" that likes control and often wants to put down the reputation of others in order to build ourselves up (the opposite of the idea of the limitless Kingdom!). Woundedness leads to agenda-ed prophecy that manipulates (sometimes subconsciously, without us even being aware that we're doing it). Wounded prophets tend to release curses accidentally, forgetting that with our prophetic provocation and challenge must come the loving opportunity for redemption. It also stops prophets from working together, which is the catastrophe of our day.

How Do You Manage Your Wounding?

Great prophecy (and leadership) is therefore not so much about your skill, technique, or even your calling. as it is about you allowing God to transform your inner world, your anxieties, fears, and insecurities. Great prophets (great leaders) know what it is to have God deal repetitively with worry, pain, heartbreak, betrayal, and rejection.

It's a fact of life that the prophet will always have to exist and operate in a somewhat "toxic" and anxious atmosphere, because people will always desire what you bring—and equally at the same time seek to undermine it. Any leader will find this to be true—that everyone wants to be led, but almost at the same time everyone wants to have a go at their leader, or help teach their leader, or "put them right."

In order to influence and prophesy with authority, the prophet must go through a process of withdrawal. The prophet in the quiet, withdrawn state learns to confront their own anxiety, and emotionally differentiate themselves from others and the anxious environments that others create. The prophet must then learn to return to the "toxic environment," maintaining relational connection and yet remaining emotionally differentiated and living out from a posture of peace. Therefore, you must never propheti-

> **Never prophesy out of reaction to your exterior circumstances, but instead prophesy from peace, because you have managed your insides well.**

cally respond to your exterior circumstances, prophesying out of reaction, but instead you prophesy from peace, because you have managed your insides. You must find a rhythm of withdrawal and engagement that keeps you emotionally well.

WHEN GOD USES YOU AND YOU GET IGNORED

Have you ever had a prophetic word that was totally ignored? Or have you given a word and the people have done almost the complete opposite of what you brought? The same thing happens in 2 Chronicles 10:1-19 (see also 1 Kings 12). Solomon is dead, and there is judgment on his family line, stemming from his sin and the sin of his father, David. God has already spoken through the prophet Ahijah, years before, that the kingdom will be broken up from the family line of Solomon (see 1 Kings 11:30-33). Then in walks Rehoboam, the family line heir, and all the people gather around. They tell him that his father Solomon has been harsh, and they beg him, "Put a light yoke on us and we will serve you."

Rehoboam takes wise prophetic counsel, and the elders again tell him to be kind. He is told that if he is, the people will follow him forever. He totally ignores it! Rehoboam doesn't listen and hangs around with his immature friends who goad him to be harsher than his father. So he turns up having listened to foolish whippersnappers and tells the people, "My father disciplined you with whips, but I will use barbed whips!"

Unsurprisingly, the people revolt, and the kingdom is divided. The lion's share of land and people becomes the new "Northern Kingdom," and the legacy of David is radically diminished. What must Rehoboam's prophetic council have thought as they watched all this! No doubt they were wincing: "If you would have just been nice, Rehoboam, we would have gone into a time of great blessing. You fool! Had you just listened to us we would all be in a better place."

Like them, I know that many times I have put my head in my hands as I've watched lives crumble, like witnessing a slow-motion car crash from afar: *"But I already prophesied you to not to do that! Look at the mess you're in now!"* The reality is that God allows people to take bad advice to see His ways outworked. God had spoken years before that there would be an ending to the line of David.

We are compelled to see the bigger history, the things that happened before we arrived. The Lord may have you speak with genuine godly intent and wisdom, but God Himself may turn the hearts of people to take bad counsel, so that they walk out judgments and plans that God has already put in place.

If this happens to you, ask God, "What is really going on here? What is Your history with these people? Am I only seeing what needs to be done right now, but, Lord, I know that You have a bigger plan?"

Be prepared to speak and for God to allow it to be ignored. Be prepared for people to go against you, even though you prophesied well, so that God can work out His justice as part of His ultimately trustworthy plan.

HONOR FOR THE PROPHET

Perhaps those prophets who are in pain have one verse that they are fond of quoting beyond all others. It is in the gospel of Luke, where Jesus says, *"'Truly I tell you,' he continued, 'no prophet is accepted in his hometown'"* (Luke 4:24 NIV). Wounded prophets wear this verse like it is a badge of honor: "Jesus was rejected so I am bound to be also, and I'm proud of my rejection." The phrase is remarkable, being quoted by the gospel writers on at least two occasions, and possibly more frequently—it certainly seems that Matthew, Mark, Luke, and John all remembered it as having been a phrase that was on the lips of Jesus whenever He was in His home region.[1]

Feeling without honor can become almost a mandate, a right to feel aggrieved, an expectation, a *chip on your shoulder*. But this proverb Jesus quotes is *not* a promise. The truth of this verse is that people will feel insecure around you because you challenge their world; the fact that they feel insecure doesn't mean that *you* must! Just because there is dishonor does not mean you need to receive it internally and react from a wounding because of it. A prophet's uncompromising truthfulness is both utterly confronting and utterly ego-deflating! Holiness is threatening to the ego.

What you prophesy is not about the prophet; *it is about the people*. It is a requisite that you can say to yourself, "I know that there is not honor here, but I will still love you and keep standing here with you, because I know your insecurities and your challenges with what Jesus is saying. Your dishonor will not impact me, because I understand this is part of my call and I have chosen to have an unoffendable heart."

It makes sense that the first place a prophet would go for support for his truthful way of thinking would be to his own family. Tragically, his family is often the very last place he can expect to find support. Having grown up with the prophet, his family are the closest people to see—and therefore suffer most—from the problems of being confronted by truthfulness and having their issues made transparent. You *might* have this dishonor happen, so choose your response.

Pep Talk Your Own Heart!

> *The Lord said to Samuel, "How long are you going to mourn for Saul, since I have rejected him as king over Israel? Fill your horn with oil and go. I am sending you to Jesse of Bethlehem because I have selected for myself a king from his sons"* (1 Samuel 16:1 CSB).

In chapter 16 of 1 Samuel, God speaks to the prophet very directly and chastises him for his personal grief. Samuel was upset and wounded because the action he had taken to anoint Saul as Israel's king had gone disastrously wrong. In essence, God quite forcefully communicates that Samuel is to get over it and let it go. The message that you can take from this moment is that you must let some things come out of your heart and become your history. Rewrite your story into a testimony and do not allow a lying pain, dishonor, or rejection to infiltrate the core of who you are.

How to Honor Prophets

Amid all this talk of rejection and wounding comes a little relief for those of us who are prophets! God gives instructions to His people in how they are to react to prophets to minimize dismissal and dishonor. So while prophets must play their part, those who hear their message must also respond within biblical frameworks. Instruction to honor the prophet is clear, both in the Old Testament and the New Testament. There is no other anointing or call that the Bible demands honor for. First, in the Old we have, "Believe His prophets and prosper." We looked at this verse (2 Chronicles 20:20) back in Chapter 10. You will "succeed," "break out," "push forward," "have sudden possession" when you take the time to honor the prophets as spokesmen for God. In this situation, Jahaziel has given King Jehoshaphat an outlandish battle strategy, so the king issues the encouragement to believe the prophet, setting the tone for us that though prophets may say some very peculiar and even unbelievable things, do not reject their strangeness or the things that look foolish to man but are, in fact, the ways of God.

Second, in the New Testament, we read of Jesus saying, "*Whoever welcomes a prophet as a prophet will receive a prophet's reward*" (Matthew 10:41 NIV). Curiously, this verse is very often quoted just before I go up to prophesy. It's something of a standard introduction, no matter what nation of the world I might be in. It begs the question, "What exactly is the prophet's reward?" Generally, it means that not only will you receive revelation, instruction, and therefore liberation from a prophet, but the greatest reward a prophet has is their ability to hear the voice of God and commune with the divine. By receiving a prophet, you open a door to a level of revelatory encounter that you personally may never have had before. Proximity to God and how He communicates is the reward the prophet can leave, far beyond anything they deliver verbally.

> **The greatest reward a prophet has is their ability to hear the voice of God and commune with the divine.**

Therefore, prophets, let us choose to flip our thinking away from expecting rejection and wounding. How about we expect to be widely honored instead? Turn your expectation around and see what it enables God to do!

ACTIVATION

Quietly sit with God and ask Him, "Am I carrying a wounding in my heart that is hindering me?"

Ask Jesus who you need to forgive. Open your hands and release the pain and wounding and allow Jesus to sit you under His waterfall of healing and life.

Ask Holy Spirit to "fly you," visually,[2] over a church or ministry that caused you pain. (This exercise will really measure your healing levels!)

Then, ask the Lord two questions:

- What is God working on for good in this organization?
- What is God excited about in this organization? Prophesy out loud what you hear.

Now ask Holy Spirit to visually "fly" you over a nation. Ask a similar two questions to before:

- What is God working on for good in this nation?
- What is God excited about in this nation? Prophesy out loud what you hear.

This activation is designed to start you in seeking God for His heart about nations but is carefully worded so that you only see the good.

CHAPTER 14

WRATH AND ANGER, LOVE AND MERCY

ULTIMATELY AS A prophet, we want to get to the place where, under the anointing, there is such a holy fear of the Lord that it dissolves in us any awareness of other people in the room and leads us to speak whatever God asks, no matter the cost.

Prophets must equally navigate the *compassion* of God, which says, "Here, this is what you don't deserve, receive it," and the *wrath* of God, which says, "This is where sin has led you and, because I am holy, here are your consequences."[1] You cannot have a prefer-ence for either the compassion or wrath of God! In other words, you cannot choose to be only a "judgment prophet" or a solely a "goodness prophet." Do you currently have a bias? If you do have a bias, you will either take the

> You cannot have a bias toward being either a "judgment prophet" or a "goodness prophet." If you do, you will take either the power or the mercy out of your prophecy.

power out of prophecy (by being too kind), or you will take the *mercy* out of prophecy (by being too harsh). Expect God to train you to be able to navigate both paths by asking you to deliver prophetic words that go against your natural inclination.

We are not our own, and we do not belong to ourselves. Your salvation does not mean that you are free to be what you want to be; it is freedom to be like Jesus! Salvation is the privilege of Christlikeness. Freedom is being set free from independence, free from your limited thinking and into the mind of Christ. God says to us, "I do not come on your terms. I do not mold Myself to your plans."

GOD'S DESCRIPTION OF HIMSELF

Exodus 34 describes another incredible encounter between Moses and Yahweh at the same mountain place as the prophet had first heard his Lord in the burning bush. As Moses crouches in the cleft of the rock and the Lord's glory passes by him, we find the first time in Scripture that God fully introduces Himself, showing the breadth and describing the whole spectrum of His nature:

> *The Lord, the Lord, the compassionate and gracious God, slow to anger, abounding in love and faithfulness, maintaining love to thousands, and forgiving wickedness, rebellion and sin. Yet he does not leave the guilty unpunished; he punishes the children and their children for the sin of the parents to the third and fourth generation* (Exodus 34:6-7 NIV).

We discover that He is slow to anger, and His preference is that His anger is temporary. This is confirmed in Psalms, where it is written, "*For his anger lasts only a moment, but his favor lasts a lifetime*" (Psalm 30:5 NIV). God's preference is for His loyal love to be eternally displayed. His preference is perpetual goodwill for His children. God's preference is to be angry only on occasion and to use that anger to push you back into living in His favor. In other words, God's wrath and anger is not uncontrolled; rather, it is purposeful and redemptive.

FIERY, HOLY GOD

As those of us in the Charismatic or Pentecostal streams of the church are usually more comfortable discussing the doctrine of the "goodness of God," I want to labor here the counter-balancing topic of the holiness and wrath of God to help realign us.

The foundations of God's throne are righteousness and justice (see Psalm 89:14; 97:2). This concept needs to take on a new understanding for the prophet. They are not foundations of love and grace, for example, or kindness and goodness, or meekness and power, or even majesty and splendor. They are very deliberately expressed to us as *righteousness and justice*. These are foundational truths. We clearly see that the cross is more about righteousness than it is about love. After all, God does not take everybody He *loves* into heaven, He takes those who have been made righteous in Jesus Christ. The (loving) work of Christ on the cross, and your belief and your acknowledgement of the need of Him as your Lord and Savior, made you the righteousness of God! "*God made him who had no sin to be sin for us, so that in him we might become the righteousness of God*" (2 Corinthians 5:21 NIV).

The story of Noah's ark should indicate to us that God is more interested in righteousness than He is in people. Let's be clear (no matter how difficult this might be to read in our comfortable, Western worldview): the Holy Bible is not a "self-help" book that

I get to use to feel uplifted about *me!* Rather it is *God's* book, His story of how He sorts out His wayward children. It is the story of His holy, fiery purity; His righteousness and justice, in which He weaves the tale together so that we can be redeemed from our unfaithful unrighteousness!

I'm not sure that most of us will have ever really wrestled with what it says in Psalm 7:11 (NIV): "*God is a righteous judge, a God who displays his wrath every day.*" The concept of a God who displays His anger every day is quite alien to us. What this means is that God is actually "okay" with a level of uncomfortableness here and now on the earth, because His value system is based on your eternal standing and getting you into a right place with Him—rather than Him feathering your nest, massaging your ego, blessing your own ideologies of Him, or backing up your cultural or political views in the present! We have made an image of God that is more like a child dressed in a police clothes costume. We have tamed Him, and in doing so we have belittled Him!

> God's value system is based on your eternal standing with Him—getting you into a right place with Him—rather than Him massaging your ego or backing up your cultural or political views!

We think the idea of God being justice, purity, and anger belongs in a bygone era, a relic best forgotten and psychologically damaging to our fragile egos. We have lost a deep sense of responsibility for personal and national character and have almost forgotten the deeply corrosive effect of sin and how much it repulses God. We have failed to take seriously what God being righteousness and justice means. Redemption via righteousness is the ultimate goal—not intellectual superiority, arrogant theology, or my own personal call.

Part of our displeasure and discomfort at this side of God is that we do not like somebody else knowing better than us! We hate in some hidden part of us the exacting standards of a higher power. We struggle with God holding a spotlight that knows us, exposes us, and calls us higher. Yet all other alternatives to a holy, pure God are even less appealing. Because He is righteous, I am pulled into an exhilarating story that takes me to places that I cannot get to alone, where in the confrontation that His holiness brings to my life I become more than just "human" and enter into the realm of a new creation.

What makes God great and what holds His Kingdom together—the very ground that founds Him and therefore underpins us—is that He is purity and holiness *without contamination*. This means that He puts things right; He makes all things right (righteousness!). It is why we can say along with Job, "*Though He slay me, yet I will trust Him*"

> **His goodness comes from His righteousness and purity.**

(Job 13:15 NKJV), because we value His higher understanding and His need for consequences.

GOD IS GOOD

"God is good all the time"—so goes the famous Christian truism. How? Why? Because He is holy and pure and without contamination. God's goodness comes from His righteousness and purity.

That means His goodness will often turn up in my life in a way I don't like!

Therefore, as prophets we look for both what is wrong and what is right. We are searching, like Jeremiah did, to understand what needs to be built up and, equally, what needs to be torn down. But what we say is *never*—and cannot ever be—a personal diatribe; the words must not originate in us. Our frustration and the "chips on our shoulders" must *never* become prophetic words in which we "give people a piece of our mind." It is not up to us. As prophets we must be continually asking how His goodness needs to be prophesied in the earth and how His holiness and justice needs to be prophesied in the earth. We are never to be assuming that we think we know what that looks like.

What Does the World Need to Hear?

The people need to know about the goodness of God but also that He sees the pain in the world. One of the Bible's most strident prophecies is found in Ezekiel 22:7-16, where the sins of Jerusalem are listed in a remarkable way: contemptuousness to parents, oppression of the foreigner, mistreating widows, despising holy things, slandering, lewd acts, violation of women, all sorts of family sexual perversion, extorting the poor, forgetting God. At the end of the list God says this:

> *I will surely strike my hands together at the unjust gain you have made and at the blood you have shed in your midst* (Ezekiel 22:13 NIV).

"I strike my hands," "I beat my fists," or "I smite my hands"— the gesture is expressive of violent agitation and great indignation! The God who calls for punishment and judgment, the God who issues urgent commands, is animated and encouraged to destroy His enemies. Have you ever seen or heard God like this? People want to know that their God is beating His fists and is responding to the world's deep issues. They want to know that He has a just response to racism, abuse, pedophilia; that He beats His fists at abortion. Prophets, we have to partner with the God who beats His fists! Cry out with me: "I want to know the God who beats His fists at the torment of rape and the shame of abuse."

Prayer

> *Oh, righteous Father, help us to find and know You as the God who beats His fists and has something to say on serious world issues. Awaken our souls from the mediocre! Save us from the prophetic words that we have spoken that are tame in modeling Your goodness and tame in modeling Your justice.*
>
> *Lord, we don't even know how to blush anymore, so shake us, give us encounters, move through Your prophetic people, and give us a voice and wake us up. Save us from our years of silence after silence after silence. Holy Spirit, help me to worship You as the God who beats His fists. In Jesus' name, amen.*

PARTNERING WITH REDEMPTION

We are now being called to partner with God in how He wants His redemption and rescuing to look, especially as it is outlined in Scripture. Six verses after God's list of Jerusalem's sins, the Lord tells Ezekiel, *"Son of man, say to the land, 'You are a land that has not been cleansed or rained on in the day of wrath'"* (Ezekiel 22:23-24 NIV).

What do we learn from this? There must be rain in this land again! We are a land that has not been cleansed or rained on by the Spirit of God and by His justice and righteousness. We are polluted because the rain of Heaven has not washed the land. We already know from the life of Elijah that there is no rain until there is a confrontation! Prophets must speak a word that is a confrontation to the ideologies that say that we can kill babies, abuse women, have sex with whom we like, lead with impurity, and prefer our nation over His Kingdom. This confrontation comes not because the prophets are hateful people, but because those ideologies kill and destroy in families and in people groups.

> **There is no rain until there is a confrontation!**

Elijah, the ultimate confronter-prophet, turns up at Mount Horeb (Sinai—yes, the place of Moses' encounters) and exclaims, "I am exceedingly zealous for the Lord of hosts" (see 1 Kings 19:10). May we cry out in the way that Elijah did!

Prayer

Oh Lord! Would You make us like that? Make us zealous for the name and the fame of You above everything! Show Your power, oh God, and make a name for Yourself. Let me partner with You in it. Let me be like Daniel—give me lion's den loyalty—that I would risk it all for Your glory. Give me the courage to speak and not be silent, the boldness to speak in the public arena!

It's Time to Get Righteously Agitated!

I believe that we need to be considerably more agitated about righteousness and justice than we currently are. The biblical prophets were agitated, prophets like Amos, who rose up and shouted, "No more, away with you!" (see Amos 5:23). Likewise, we are to be agitated and violent against the principalities and powers. We have only played with the power of God when it comes to taking on the demons in the higher realms.

Let's return to Ezekiel and read what he says about the religious leaders:

> *Her priests do violence to my law and profane my holy things; they do not distinguish between the holy and the common; they teach that there is no difference between the unclean and the clean; and they shut their eyes to the keeping of my Sabbaths, so that I am profaned among them. Her officials within her are like wolves tearing their prey; they shed blood and kill people to make unjust gain* (Ezekiel 22:26-27 NIV).

The priests and officials of Israel are like the church today. We are surrounded by compromise in the church (at least in the non-persecuted West), so much so that many of its leaders cannot stand with Jesus and cannot stand against the moral corruption of our day—because of how corrupt they are themselves. The church's leaders cannot call a nation into order because they are in so much personal disarray.

Of course, we do need to be those who love our enemies and forgive those who harm us, but we also are mandated to *stand for truth*. Prophets confront the ideologies that say "God is not holy" and declare that who He is must be known again. Always leaning into awe, wonder, and a complete belief in whatever God says (with the accompanying courage to say it) will lead us to break our agreement with cynicism, small thinking, self-obsession, and pessimism.

Still in Ezekiel 22—and now he turns on the prophets!

> *Her prophets whitewash these deeds for them by false visions and lying divinations. They say, "This is what the Sovereign Lord says"—when the Lord has not spoken* (Ezekiel 22:28 NIV).

I don't even think that Ezekiel is referring to willfully false prophets, demonic diviners, or evil sorcerers here. He is talking about the prophets who pander to the people, massage egos, and water down messages to sound more pleasing. These are prophets whose swords are no longer sharp!

Prophets whose swords are no longer sharp pander to the people, water down messages, and massage egos!

The reason that I keep returning to Ezekiel 22 is because I want you to get a feel for the call of the prophet who is a truth teller, no matter what the cost is. I want you to see how *wired for truth* we need to be. We are to be bold truth tellers, as God leads us. Two final verses:

> *I looked for someone among them who would build up the wall and stand before me in the gap on behalf of the land so I would not have to destroy it, but I found no one. So I will pour out my wrath on them and*

consume them with my fiery anger, bringing down on their own heads all they have done, declares the Sovereign Lord (Ezekiel 22:30-31 NIV).

"But I found no one." Oh, the heartache of this set of verses, as God goes searching for a co-laborer and finds no one. God is scouring the earth—looking, wanting to appoint people who will stand in the gap and speak up. He is searching for those who will say boldly dangerous things like, "If you want to get past me, you are going to have to kill me! I'm not moving from my call and from telling the truth." Is that a spirit that we have in the prophetic movement today?

The Lord is seeking to raise up a house of the prophets who will courageously contend and speak into the issues of nations without a trace of fear. Now is the time to break off the things that keep you small. It is the moment to immediately line up with your call and to wear the mantle God wants to give you!

Prayer

Father, show me more of who You are and how You think, that I might become the voice You need in the earth today. In Jesus' name, amen.

CHAPTER 15

Prophets and Relationships

Submission Leads to Greater Authority

To be trusted by God as one who can bring both messages of wrath and compassion requires a profoundly yielded life-style. Another word for *yielded* is *submitted*. Now, I know that to modern sensibilities the concept of submission is incredibly loaded and unfashionable, so let me give you a positive example to explain how it can work for the good of everyone.

David and I have a *mission* before God to reveal the voice of God to the nations. Each of our staff teams also has their own very important personal, group, and departmental missions, but these are all *sub*-missions to the overall mission of our collective house ("revealing the voice of God to the nations"). Our job as leaders, therefore, is not to "lord it" over them about the one main mission, but rather to underpin them and support them in their missions and responsibilities, and to enable them to be fully alive in doing so. There is no need for crushing control, which means instead that our hearts can beat toward helping their projects and passions fit as a *submission of the main mission*.

It benefits everyone, then, if we pour considerable resources, training, and serving from us to them, so that they can thrive in their mission. It's a liberating recipe for growth! But if their mission cannot ever become a submission, they are probably in the wrong tribe.

We all must hold in tension the hierarchical structure of the family of God, where leaders (just like fathers and mothers) are put in place for a reason, while at the same time submitting back and forward, one to another, for the purposes of growing, sharpening, and moving onward from glory to glory. On occasion, our greatest life lessons are taught to us by our children.

Generally, if you think that you only have a *co*-mission rather than a *sub*-mission in all your relationships, you are likely to have a wrong partnership with independence. All of us need places of submission in our lives. Independent, self-governed voices—those who do not relate to others well—are never sharpened enough to be useful. Usefulness as a prophet comes in boldness and courage, in intimacy with God that understands what He wants said, and also in and through the relationships that sharpen.

> **Usefulness as a prophet also comes in and through relationships that sharpen.**

We must be brave enough to ask an honest set of "independence testing" questions! Such as:

- How closely do I let leaders speak into my life? Remember that your identity is often more known to your leaders than it is to you!

- How often do I put myself in accountable relationships, into places of sharpening, where I yield and surrender to another's opinion?

- How well do I take correction from others?

- Do I have a track record of walking away from relationships after being sharpened, or do I have the maturity to stay in the room?

- On a scale from one to ten, how teachable am I?

- Have I listened to people who want the best for me, or have I become offended with how they approached me rather than being grateful that they took the time to speak into my life?

If you answered too many of these questions with forceful independence or even a subtle, passive aggressive kickback, you know it is time to reframe your relationships.

Anecdotally, from conversations with other church leaders, I have found that most people will leave a church because they had zero ability to either sit in correction (or even mild challenge) or were unable to yield to leadership taking them somewhere that they had not thought up for themselves. But is it not the point of leadership that it takes you somewhere you cannot get to by yourself? Otherwise, you wouldn't need to be led in the first place. Our independence sadly means that we often don't stay in relationships that require us to hear truth.

I was surprised some years ago, when teaching in a room of under-25-year-olds, to discover that most of them had no understanding of what biblical authority or submission actually meant. The *zeitgeist* had so mauled and informed them that they had almost no cultural understanding of absolute truth or the sweet place of tucking in under authority. Take some time to ask yourself, "What do I understand by the concept of being under authority?"

"I am a man under authority," uttered the Roman centurion in Matthew 8. He was dialoguing with Jesus over the healing of a paralyzed servant in his home, recognizing that he did not require Jesus to visit the suffering man in person and that he only needed Jesus to command healing from a distance. The centurion understood that Jesus had sufficient authority to command and impact change, without having to be physically present. The centurion, who was well versed in the Roman military's well-used systems of empowering authority, knew that if he honored and tucked himself under the strength of one greater than himself, that same greatness would respond to his honor and produce what he could not produce for himself.

> **True authority is used to protect, nurture, and fight for those in its care.**

True authority is used to protect, nurture, and fight for those in its care. True authority will go to war to fight a battle ahead of time, so that you don't even have to face it! Sitting under true authority is like having a guardian and wall of protection around about you. In the gospel account, Jesus is amazed at the centurion's faith because not many understand the breakthrough that comes from believing in, and following, those who have been given greater authority than you have. Great authority can catapult you into places that you cannot get yourself.

> *Obey your leaders and submit to them, for they keep watch over your souls as those who will give an account. Let them do this with joy and not with grief, for this would be unprofitable for you* (Hebrews 13:17 NASB95).

Obedience to leadership is mandated in this scripture. There's a specific call on the life of a leader to guard the souls of those in their care, and leadership will have to give an account for the souls of the sheep that have been assigned to them. Therefore, there is a watchfulness that leaders must have—and when there is major kickback against their leading, it causes them grief and lessens their spiritual power. If you are leaderless, you are in an exposed place. It is time for us to "gang up" on the enemy! It is time to understand the power and breakthrough that is available to us collectively—not only when we coalesce as peers, but when we find our place in the leadership structure that God has ordained for us. We must learn to let ourselves be sharpened, and then we can enter a new level of holiness and fear of the Lord. Truth might nip and sting for a season, but it grows freedom in us over the long term.

LISTEN TO GOD ABOUT YOUR OWN LIFE

To remain healthy, well, and prophesying with unbiased clarity, prophets must hear from God regularly about their own lives! It is quite normal for a prophet to hear from God for everybody else in their world, but then to really wrestle with hearing God for themselves. This can trip the prophet up because when they do prophesy, they can accidentally release "self-words" (rather than corporate words for the wider body) that never got stewarded in the private place. Partly this error comes because the call of the prophet is a lifestyle of leadership, and those with vocational roles can easily forget what it is to be a sheep themselves. We can learn how to hear God but forget to learn to receive from God. This requires a posturing of the heart to sit openly and transparently, with all guards down, giving the Lord the space to iron out your issues.

Perhaps most of how God speaks we do not perceive. Most of what He asks us to do we miss. Therefore, when we are advancing into a new day, with new anointings to work with, there must be a greater personal attentiveness given to His voice that can be applied to our own rhythms, heart, and internal dialogue. It is a requisite standard for the prophet to look and listen all the time for His voice—in nature, wind, rain, sunshine, and people—with all senses alive to Him, and to sit with our chests ripped open to Him so that He might mark us deeply. As a prophet I must know how He sounds as a relational God, first through His relationship with me!

WE DON'T HEAR BECAUSE WE DON'T OBEY

Why then are we not hearing from God more often, and in greater detail, for ourselves—and only then after that for others? It is because we are dull to it! As a child in the temple, Samuel answers God with the famous phrase, *"Speak, Lord, for your servant is listening"* (1 Samuel 3:9 NIV). I grew up with the old King James translation of this verse, which had Samuel saying, *"Your servant hears."* But the Hebrew שֹׁמֵעַ somea is better translated (as it is in more modern translations) as "is listening." This has a meaning beyond simply "hears." It implies "to hear—with the intent to obey."[1]

Feasibly a reason why we don't hear God as much as we would like is because we don't have the intent to obey what He tells us, and so He doesn't speak to us. If you hear *and disobey* that would put you in rebellion to God and *"rebellion is as the sin of witchcraft"* (1 Samuel 15:23 KJV), so God would rather not talk than have you under that curse. He loves you so much that He stops speaking so that you don't end up in rebellion and witchcraft!

God needs to trust you. Friends tell friends secrets, and prophetic ministry is a matter of friendship with God. Therefore, it is time to ask yourself some more soul-searching questions:

> If your prophetic ear has been dulled, then learn how to listen with the intent to obey.

- Have I dulled myself to Your voice, God, because I have not obeyed when You spoke?
- Do I love our interactions and encounters but do not apply the revelation when it raises a challenge to me?

The Bible doesn't literally say, "If you love Me, you will worship Me." Nor for that matter does it say, "If you love Me, you will heal people," or, "If you love Me, you will pray for people," or, "If you love Me, you will have a great ministry." The command of Jesus is, *"If you love Me, you will obey Me."*

BE TRUE TO YOURSELF

If I am to be a useful voice and a bold voice, then I need to begin with my own heart. Perhaps Shakespeare sums it up best:

This above all: to thine own self be true, And it must follow, as the night the day, Thou canst not then be false to any man.[2]

When I am true to me, I can speak truth to others. If the world needs a truth revelation, then *I* need a truth revolution! If my mouth is a weapon of truth and power to the world, then my heart must also undergo truth surgery.

As the emerging prophets become prophets of power, they must be truthful about themselves. Truth and power must rise together. Did God perhaps withhold power from us because we weren't being truthful or operating in the John 16 "spirit of truth"? *"You are in error because you do not know the Scriptures or the power of God"* (Matthew 22:29 NIV). This verse packs a punch to the gut because in it Jesus admonishes us that we neither know truth, nor do we know power. Jesus pulls truth and power together as both needing to be present. The irony is we are usually only too aware of our powerless state but remain completely ignorant of our truthless state. We think that we have grasped truth and that our church framework helps us protect it, but we have failed to realize that God's truth is so profound that we grow into it, and it continually shapes us.

PRAYER

Cry out for God to do what He did in the days of Jeremiah:

God write truth on my heart! Tattoo my insides with Your reality; mark me with truth. May truth define me and truth-telling own me. Lord, the Psalms tell me that, "You desire truth in the innermost being" (Psalm 51:6 NASB). You desire that my insides would get real, that in me there would be no self-deception, no overinflated notions, no fake news, no dressed-up reports of who I am and what needs to be changed about me. No fairy tales, exaggerations, or distortions. No misrepresenting myself to myself.

I confess that I dress up for others and manipulate my own image so that others can celebrate me. I repent of my desire for "likes" of my status to be ever present and plentiful! But much more than this, oh Lord, in the secret place may I not lie to me about me and believe my own PR. May I instead have genuine authenticity and plain-talking exactness about who I am, how I am doing, and what is really happening in my world.

"You desire truth in the innermost being"—Jesus, please banish my internal myths and enable me, by Your Spirit, to tell truth to my own heart.

Father, I repent for not actioning what You have already spoken and thus I became dull of hearing. God, would You speak to me? I want to listen as one who has the intent to obey. In Jesus' name, amen.

CHAPTER 16

WHAT MAKES A FALSE PROPHET?

WHEN I AM teaching introductory classes about the prophetic gift there is nearly always a question from one of the nervous participants along the lines of, "What if I prophesy wrongly or inaccurately—does that make me a 'false prophet'?" Most beginners in the gift wrestle to distinguish the voice of God from their own internal monologue. Layer this with perhaps some limited biblical knowledge and/or a lack of linguistic ability that might struggle to apply the English language to the voice of the divine, and we can probably surmise that a reasonable amount of prophecy from novices poorly reflects what God is actually trying to communicate!

Nevertheless, in these entry-level classes we are always careful to reassuringly respond that, "No, wrong words make you a *poor* prophet, not a false prophet." We make it clear to our inexperienced students: false prophets are out to see the church utterly destroyed. If you want to see the church completely annihilated and under demonic control, then, yes, you are very likely a Jezebelic false prophet! The aim in giving this comfort to beginners in the gift is to empower them to have a go at prophecy in a safe environment and to iron out, with us, their early-years stumbling blocks to prophetic utterance.

However, in the more senior classes that we teach to emerging prophets, the definition of "false prophet" we give runs a much narrower line, where persistent failures in the waters of poor prophecy that cause and culminate in an unrepentant and repetitive leading astray of the people, will earn you the unfortunate title of "false prophet." Perhaps not a false prophet by Jezebel's standards, but nevertheless a "false" prophet in the sense of single-mindedly and continually leading people away from the core of the word of the Lord, and from Jesus Christ Himself. Maybe the term "unfaithful prophet" is a more accurate term to describe this kind of erroneous behavior, where a person's heart genuinely loves Jesus, but they are flawed in how they keep outworking "revelation." (Conceivably, there might be a sliding scale downward, from poor prophecy to unfaithful prophet to false prophet. And that goes for the other fivefold gifts too!) Whatever we call them, the sad fact is that the unfaithful prophet usually does untold damage before they are stopped in their tracks.

CHARACTERISTICS OF UNFAITHFUL PROPHETS

1. Self-Promotion

Self-promotion is when you prophesy for personal advantage, redefining God for personal agenda. Most prophets will know what stirs a congregation up and can play this to their benefit. At its core it is feel-good revelation to get people on your side and liking you, promising all sorts of advancement and financial reward from God into their lives, with no tempering of holiness or process. It's introducing ourselves more than we introduce God—you know that you're on thin ice when congregations are hearing more about your product and resources than what God is actually saying. (Included under this category would be the publishing of "click-bait words" for fame on social media, just so that you rise in notoriety.)

Once this spirit of self-preference over God preference has taken hold it will lead to a violation of good prophetic protocol and best practice, releasing words without due process. The word will sound good to you, and you know it will make you look great (or get you views), and so you give in to the temptation of releasing it without the due diligence of submission, testing, and editing.

This category of unfaithful prophecy also includes political preference over God preference and national preference over Kingdom preference. In this, our personal biases lead us away from promoting God's words and into promoting our own preferred or inherited ideologies.

In general, good protocol dictates that 1) words for churches go to church platforms, 2) words for leaders go to leaders (these are not often for public consumption), and 3) words for nations can be more publicly shared. Therefore, learn to manage your prophetic urgency and your need to be seen, by rightly appropriating words and sitting on your personal desire for visibility. You have nothing to prove—we all know everybody can hear the voice of God (see 1 Corinthians 14:31). It's not impressive to hear God, but it is impressive to steward those words righteously. In Scripture we see that major words for governmental leaders often came on the back of preestablished relational lines of communication. For example, Daniel was summoned, Joseph was recommended and called upon, and Micaiah was invited in. If you don't have access to the political leaders, pray it instead. Ask God the reasons why you don't yet have access to deliver the word: are you trustworthy in motive with not wanting your own name known? So note this well: if you don't have relational access to a leader, the word is for you to pray, not for you to show off.

> It's not impressive to hear God but it is impressive to steward those words righteously.

2. *Distorting the Message*

Remember, God is equally wrath and love. If you cannot navigate both, you will bring an incomplete representation of God. When you do this, you lead people away from the fullness of who He is. Distortion is willfully misrepresenting God to be either harsher, or kinder, than He has communicated with you through His word. I would urge you to ask some trusted people what it's like to be on the receiving end of your revelation, because it is easy to get caught up in a moment and to misunderstand the impression that you are giving of what God has said.

> Ask some trusted people what it's like to be on the receiving end of your revelation.

3. *Releasing Fear and Anxiety*

Releasing or putting atmospheres into the room that are not the Kingdom of God is another sign of an unfaithful prophet. John writes, "*Dear friends, do not believe every spirit, but test the spirits to see whether they are from God, because many false prophets have gone out into the world*" (1 John 4:1 NIV). We are to test the spirits of the prophet. This is noteworthy—we are not just to weigh the words (see 1 Corinthians 14:29). In testing the spirits, we test the motivation of the speaker, we test the atmosphere or spiritual feeling that they have created. Did their word come from the Spirit of God, their human spirit, or a demonic spirit?

If you prophesy from a fear base, a wrong judgment base, or a base of over-realized compassion, your "spirit" or motivation will not be wholly pure. Be aware that you can show unsanctified compassion and even speak mercy where God is not speaking mercy. Therefore, when we listen to words, we weigh and judge what they do in the room. Did they motivate us and call us into the right place, or, for example, did they just drop us into unsanctified fear and tension?

> **When you release words from the wrong motivation you rob the people of God's best.**

When you release words from the wrong motivation, you rob the people of God's best. God always has our best interests at heart over the long haul, even during our trials. Even if there is the need to release a word about the consequences of sin, there must always be some redemption woven into it. I have heard prophetic words that are right in their content and wrong in their motivation, meaning that they will have created an ungodly response in the hearts of the listener, despite their accuracy. Therefore, the prophet must ask what the will of God is. Your question must be, "What is God's best here?" and not, "What is my best outcome for this room?" The right attitude coming from you the prophet will enable challenging words to be received. After all, you want your listener to be motivated to follow God with relative ease.

4. *Problematic Altar Calls*

My definition of a "problematic altar call" is when a congregation rushes to the front to receive an impartation from the speaker rather than from God. A prophet should not lead people to themselves or exclusively and consistently to the impartation that they can give, but to God. We seem to have developed a strange and disturbing church culture of believing that it is the speaker who has what we want or need! We must always be very clear that prophetic words and messages do not originate in the prophet. They originate with God, and they are given to connect people back to Him.

St. Augustine wrote, "You have made us for yourself, O Lord, and our hearts are restless until they rest in you."[1] Have we created restless people by our ministry style, which brings men to us and establishes the repetitive, habitual need to receive from a person, leading to the modern phenomenon of "conference junkies"?

Have we got sucked into mixing up an addictive recipe that contains a

> **Prophetic messages do not originate in the prophet. They are from God, given to connect people back to Him.**

sprinkle of inspiration, a dash of theology, a touch of the Bible, and a whole lot of sweet personality? Leaders, speakers, and ministers, have you ever asked yourself, "What motivates people to come forward at the end of our meetings? Why do we call them to the front?" If we answer ourselves honestly, it is probably more often for self-validation reasons (to make us feel that we've done a good job) rather than for any deep stirring from God Himself in that moment.

5. Stale Words

Traveling ministers often exhaustedly prophesy the same thing over and over again because they lack the preparation time to receive and interpret a fresh word. Admittedly, God sometimes has us carry words for an extended season, but one of my personal pet hates is someone telling me of a word or dream they had that is many years old. It is usually quite apparent from this that the sharer has not recognized that the timeframe for implementation of the revelation has long ago expired. Watch that your words are not out of season!

> *Even the stork in the sky knows her appointed seasons, and the dove, the swift and the thrush observe the time of their migration. But my people do not know the requirements of the Lord* (Jeremiah 8:7 NIV).

Be punctual to your season. Understand that seasons change—and can change very rapidly. It's why Peter the apostle talks about being "established in present truth" (see 2 Peter 1:12 NKJV)—truth is always true, but God certainly seems to have varying truth emphases across different seasons—and also why Ecclesiastes tells us that there is a time and season for every activity under heaven. Sometimes we embrace, sometimes we refrain! (See Ecclesiastes 3:1,5.)

A preacher speaking from yesterday's revelation can lead us into methodology, stuckness, and boredom! Stale words become a trap to us—we get out of the pace of God and fail to realize what is required from us today. They cause us to lose our edge and pull us into protecting where we are, rather than motivating us to embrace advancing. Prophetic people recognize stale communication by the level of frustration it awakens internally—even though there may be nothing intrinsically wrong with what is being said. You can listen to considerable quantities of preaching and prophesying, and the content rings true, yet you still find yourself unnerved by it. This is frequently because it is not in step with what God is doing in the present moment.

> From the tribe of Issachar, there were 200 leaders of the tribe with their relatives. All these men understood the signs of the times and knew the best course for Israel to take (1 Chronicles 12:32 NLT).

Issachar has always been understood to be the prophetic tribe because of their understanding of the timings and rhythms of the calendar for the nation of Israel. A mature prophetic voice will continually be seeking to keep their people up to date with what God is saying in that present moment, as well as being able to secure a people's future by understanding how to frame their

Stale words trap us out of the pace of God, failing to realize what is required from us today.

forth-telling. Take time to ask God if what you are carrying is still fresh and has not expired.

6. Prophesying Prayers

Turning our intercession into a *"thus says the Lord"* (prophesying our prayers) has led whole people groups to follow what one person (or more) earnestly desired, rather than responding to what God was saying. This doesn't always happen for nefarious reasons or because of ulterior motives and can often come about inadvertently or by an accidental overshoot. So much of our time together *should* be spent pouring ourselves out in prayer, and it takes great maturity and discipline to only pray as the Spirit leads, mirroring the standards and plans of the Kingdom of Jesus in our intercession. However, our prayers frequently fall into the category of our own demands and desires, where we pray through *our* preferences, not pausing to listen to the Lord. We fail to realize (or admit) that our preferences are not always either what God is saying or what He wants us to pray.

Prophets must be very guarded and extremely careful in identifying the difference between a word of prophecy and a word in prayer. *Both* should be what God wants, but often a word of prophecy is what God is saying and a word in prayer is what *we* are personally desiring. For example, you can, by all means, bring the political candidate that you desire to be elected before the Lord in prayer, but do not

> **Prophets must be very careful to identify the difference between a word of prophecy and a word in prayer.**

make that a prophetic utterance! Just because you petition it in prayer does not mean that God wants it or will do it. Prophets, we must keep ourselves to a high standard, where we are clinically clear in our communication, outlining either that we are prophesying or that we are praying, with no room for any ambiguity.

7. Prophesying Other People's Words

"Therefore…I am against the prophets who steal from one another words supposedly from me." So declares the Lord in Jeremiah 23:30 (NIV). *The Message* interprets this verse vividly:

> *I've had it with the "prophets" who get all their sermons secondhand from each other. Yes, I've had it with them. They make up stuff and then pretend it's a real sermon.*

As we can clearly see, the Bible is very strong on the error of echoing prophecy! Even if a senior, established prophet has brought a marvelous word that resonates with our own spirit and we judge it to be a true word, we still must hold ourselves to a standard where we source what God is saying to *us*. God gives different revelation to each prophet to form a woven collective tapestry of all our parts. Revelation is entrusted into personality types that can deliver its differing styles and approaches. What He puts into one prophet, He will rarely put into a second prophet in

> What He puts into one prophet, He will rarely put into a second in the same way.

exactly the same way. Words certainly will join up and overlap but are rarely ever identical.

Therefore, watch out that you do not become lazy, scared of getting it wrong, or overly enamored with another prophet's approach to the point that we withhold the part that is our portion—and therefore mandatory for us to bring.

Be Faithful to Your Portion

If we have inadvertently stepped into any of these seven unfaithful behavior patterns, it is time to take some time out and ask God to reframe how we disseminate and steward the revelation He has for us to bring. We want to be faithful to our portion and found faithful to the call, not found accidentally unfaithful by slipping into sloppy habits or modeling what we see around about us. A.W. Tozer puts it well in this edit based on one of his prayers:

Tozer's Prayer[2]

I am a prophet—not a promoter. I am a prophet, not a people impresser. Let me never be a slave to crowds. Save me from bondage to things or people. May I wrestle with principalities and powers and rulers of darkness, not the opinions of men or my call. You have given me a task that is awesome in a grave and perilous age. I will not spend my time deploring my weakness or focus on my unfitness for the work.

Save me from compromise, imitation of others, and judging success by size and popularity. I will not waste my days. Your will is sweeter than anything else in my life.

Save me from myself and all the injuries I do myself while trying to bless others. May I only go in Your strength till I am old, and my time has come.

CHAPTER 17

BECOMING A
USEFUL VOICE

IN MANY OF the prophetic words we give we have no idea what we're talking about—we only see in part! (See 1 Corinthians 13:9-12.) Therefore, we often do not understand the context into which we speak. The job is to be faithful to the part you do have, which means you will often wonder how the prophetic word is going to be applied. Some of the imagery that God shows you will mean everything to the recipient and very little to you. To know that the prophetic call is set up for you to not fully understand is a very strange thing indeed.

Nevertheless, this shouldn't completely surprise us. Prophetic and indeed Christian leadership is a peculiar thing. When it is done well, it runs almost counter to everything the world has told us. The world says, "Look good! Create yourself by accumulating wealth, experiences, and travels—and then broadcast your life to an audience who will tell you how awesome you are!" But the gospel of the Kingdom jars against this. Jesus said to His followers in the gospel of Luke, "*Whoever wants to be my disciple must deny themselves and take up their cross daily and follow me"* (Luke 9:23 NIV).

Mature prophets can keep standing in situations and repetitively speak things forth, all the while having limited clarity or no real feel for what they're speaking into. It doesn't always feel good. In fact, on occasion it is quite draining! This consistently pushes you to deny yourself the need to be celebrated so that whatever God wants is communicated. Sometimes you have to say the hard things, the strange things, the abnormal and atypical things, the uncomfortable things.

THREE CATEGORIES OF PROPHETIC WORDS

What we prophesy usually fits into one of three categories:

1. *Prophetic Generalities*

First, we speak our words, our agenda, and our ideas, giving *prophetic generalities*. God hasn't spoken in the moment, but we, the prophet, can pull together a reasonable Scripture verse or idea that might be generally useful. Things like, "You're coming into a fresh understanding of how much God loves you," is usually always true, and most prophets will know this without actually hearing God say anything. It is picking biblical truths, tailored as best *we* think the person needs to hear.

This style of revelation (if we can even call it that) is not always as dreadful as it sounds, as it encapsulates good ideas, sensible words, and possibly the best strategy that we have on a matter. It would be better to couch it in opinion, so you would say, "I think if you did this _____ you would see a turnaround." It is wisdom without revelation. Listen carefully to revelation in the future and you might be surprised just how much of what we in the church call the "word the Lord" is basically just this approach!

2. Prophetic Words We Understand and Like

The second category of prophecy is when we speak God's words, we like them, and they feel like "good words" to our own spirits. The word "sits right" with us. *We understand the prophecy.*

These are the "flying high" moments of revelation, when you feel joyfully alive as the words coming out of your mouth are words that you want to be there, and they are full of wisdom and revelation!

Pleasingly, they make you look good and afterward you think you did a great job and everyone thinks that you're epic. Because of the considerable "feel good" that this type of prophecy generates, it is all too easy for most

> **Being obedient to bring some words will mean dying to yourself in the communication of them.**

people to stay in this style of revelation. After all, why would you willingly choose any other style of prophecy unless you robustly feared the Lord?

3. Prophetic Words We Don't Like

Finally, there is the type of revelation that means we speak God's words, and *we don't like them*—they taste bitter to us. We don't understand them—they make us look strange. There is an immediate awareness that to be obedient will mean some degree of dying to yourself in the communication of them. You don't get to pick and choose what you release, and you don't get to add your opinion to the word. No one wants to hear that!

This is not just a matter of bringing "justice" or "consequences" words. In fact, on occasions it is quite the opposite. Once, God asked me to prophesy over a church leader whom I knew for a fact was in sexual sin. At the time I was still reeling from the sudden disclosure of his quite considerable history of perversion that had come to light just twenty-four hours prior. Sexual sin demons oozed out of every pore of him! As I stood at the front of his church, wondering how to navigate this with his congregation, God asked me to prophesy, calling him "pure," "spotless," and "righteous" before Him.

As the Lord told me this, the internal wrestle within me was immense! "But those words are not true, Jesus! They are not even *close* to being accurate!" I argued. I knew that I would look a fool if I said those things out loud.

I took the microphone, closed my eyes, clenched my fist, pressed deeply into the Holy Spirit, and said, "God calls you pure, spotless, and righteous." The gasps from the congregation were audible. I looked like a crazy fool who was only massaging the leader's ego and securing him in position. The rest of the day was just unpleasant because I subsequently couldn't get the congregation's buy-in to anything else I had to say!

Several years passed and I was attending a large conference in another part of the country. Out of the blue, this leader and his wife happened to appear, standing beside me at the front during the worship. Let me tell you, he was *unrecognizable!* He was in every way pure, spotless, and righteous. My jaw dropped as I did a double take to check it was the same person, and, as I did so,

God whispered in my ear, "You did that—you created his future all those years ago, by giving him something to step into."

On more than one occasion God has asked me to tell a church or ministry that He is closing them down and removing His grace, even when every fiber of my being wanted to speak life and call them back into fullness! Perhaps one of the most challenging moments of obedience came when God asked me to publicly tell a minister that he had not ever been called to ministry and so he was in the wrong job.

The soul searching one must do over these kinds of words is almost indescribable, where disobedience feels like a choice you might never recover from, but equally, obedience feels like relational suicide. In this particular situation with the minister-who-should-never-have-been, his wife screamed and fell to her knees, publicly crying out, "We knew it! We knew it! We just didn't know what to do!" Incredibly, despite my apprehension, they were grateful!

How to Deliver Difficult Words

Best practice, generally, is to sit in very private rooms to deliver these sorts of words. On the rare occasions that they must be made publicly, it is usually only because the people involved have already been told by God, repetitively, over years, but have consistently chosen disobedience. When the word makes it to the public domain it is, in reality, an extreme mercy of God to give a final opportunity for redress and reframing.

In a split second, you can feel somewhat hijacked by God, but this quickly gives way to the reward of hearing His voice and being trusted by Him.

In one situation, midway through preaching about something else, God suddenly gave me the name of a ministry that I did not previously know existed and asked me to prophesy that they were, "Ishmael and not Isaac." After delivering the word I could feel, all at once, a mix of things: the pleasure of the Father, the swirl of others' human emotions, my own personal wrestle of, "Did I go about it the right way?" and the thoughts about future personal reputational damage. However, putting something in the public domain like that is utterly transparent and rightly gives everyone the ability to weigh and test the word and, in cases like this, to discern their alignment to the ministry involved. This is an incredibly important process, giving us the opportunity to assess if what we're doing is what, and how, God wants things done.

I used to ask God why He works like this, but He alone knows. Now I fear Him rightly, and not man, and in the anointing I understand that my life is not my own. Neither is my reputation, and I know that the prophetic anointing always gives people choices and provokes decision-making. The prophet in Scripture is never about harmony but is always about righteousness. This takes years to settle into *and must always be underpinned by an absolute driving passion for the people of God and a love for His church.*

> You can feel hijacked by God, but this quickly gives way to the reward of hearing His voice and being trusted by Him.

We want to be an echo of God. When we are not, what it tends to generate is harsh, rude, or deliberately shocking opinions, just to stand out for standing out's sake, along with self-generated, man-made, spiritual visions that God never gave you—because you wanted to look "cutting edge."

Sometimes I have prophesied and thought, "Wow, what a great word for that person—God You are really blessing them!" and God has replied to me, "That was a justice word! It would have been a different prophecy had they not been needing to reap what they sowed." What I had prophesied, and thought was good, was actually *much less* than they would have received at another time. Every listener would have celebrated what God was saying in the moment had they not had an eye to see what God was doing behind the scenes.

BOLDNESS

It is emphatically undeniable that the prophet requires a divinely generated, courageous boldness (not rudeness)! You have to get happy at not holding back in response to what God is saying through you.

How is your courage and boldness? I find that—at the entry level—most prophetic types have so wrangled and battled to come to terms with navigating their frustration of the *status quo* that they struggle to be courageously life-giving in their words. As a result, they lean into a kind of frustrated telling-off instead!

It is a lifelong journey to become a useful voice—finding your words, tone, heart setting, language, platform, and sound. It is a process to lose your fear (but not become belligerent in the process) so that the fear of God can replace it. Mantles of divinely generated, courageous boldness must come forth and be picked up and worn by emerging prophets. Of course, it's not just a matter of loudness or how strongly you say something, it's more nuanced than that. Sometimes you must prophesy in a whisper—get comfortable in the peculiarity of the call!

Get comfortable that you are not going to be popular in some moments. Not that people will always be raging against you as if you are at war with them; they are simply uncomfortable with the challenge you present. I have lost count of the number of platforms that I have stood on and said, "God, do I really need to say that?"—and all that was being said was relatively normal. But it was such a provocation neverthe-less—because *that's the anointing*. Never underestimate how your anointing provokes, even before you have opened your mouth! A prophet can walk into a room in total, dignified silence and still irritate others because the anointing provokes change. Prophets comfort the afflicted and afflict the comfortable.[1]

> Prophets comfort the afflicted and afflict the comfortable.

CHAPTER 18

THE SECOND WAVE

IN 2018, DR. TIM HAMON, son of Bishop Dr. Bill Hamon (founder of the modern-day prophetic movement),[1] released a word at Christian International's Florida headquarters, prophesying that it was the beginning of the "second wind of the prophetic movement."[2] He preached from Ezekiel 37, the prophet's open vision of the valley of dry bones, and he drew the attention of all of us who were there to verse seven:

> Ezekiel does prophesy [to the dry bones] as instructed: "So I prophesied as I was commanded; and as I prophesied, there was a noise, and suddenly a rattling; and the bones came together, bone to bone. Indeed, as I looked, the sinews and the flesh came upon them, and the skin covered them over; but there was no breath in them."

Dr. Tim continued:

> I see the bones, sinews, flesh, skin, but where is the breath? The problem is there's no breath. Now this is troubling to me because God told Ezekiel to prophesy to the dry bones. Listen to what He

tells Ezekiel to prophesy, "The Lord says to you, surely I will cause a breath to enter into you…" and He says, "and I will put breath in you, and you shall live." Well, that didn't happen. Verse 8 ends clearly, "There was no breath." It's the only thing the Lord said twice, and when the Lord starts repeating Himself it's for emphasis. So, He emphasizes the breath, but the breath does not come.

The point that Dr. Tim went on to make in his memorable message was that prophetic people are in a very similar place. He said:

> We've been gathering with a lot of noise (bones to bones), we have been linking up (sinew to sinew), we've been imparting strength and power by equipping and training (flesh and muscles), and we've been covering them, defending them, making them whole, and teaching integrity (skin). But the Lord is saying there's really not breath [ruach, "spiritual breath"—the Spirit of God] in it.

Then, as he received this revelation about Ezekiel 37 and the modern prophetic movement, Dr. Tim recalled four significant prophetic words for Christian International given at an event in 2016:

- First, Barbara Yoder prophesied, "I understand this is the time of birthing a new prophetic movement…the greatest years you ever had and more miracles."

- Later, Cindy Jacobs declared, "It's time…to go to a new prophetic level with power and authority. And more miracles than we have ever seen."

- Next, Dutch Sheets said, "God is releasing a new prophetic mantle [on Christian International]. It will cause us to be 'wind people.' And you will be like eagles that will lock into the wind of God and soar over the storms with greater authority as you enter into the new wind of God."

- Finally, Bishop Bill Hamon also declared at the same event that a "second wave of the prophetic was coming."

Dr. Tim explains his revelation:

So, here's what's happening: Ezekiel has prophesied, the word of God comes, all the bones come together, they've been equipped, covered, and defended and prepared except they're not moving the way they need to move yet, or at all. I don't like the idea that this is where we are at now. We've been equipping, preparing, making strong, putting together, assembling together all those people and now we want to be an army.

We're in the next phase. We're in the next wind. You know when you need the second wind is when you run out of breath. When the breath has been expelled and you don't know where the next breath is coming from. That second wind is here and here's how it works, you prophesy to the first wind and you say, "Come alive! Come alive and empower us to stand up like an army!"

In Ezekiel 37, a second moment of life and breath was required for the dry bones to arise as an army who are on the offensive.

As I listened to Dr. Tim Hamon that day, I believe that something remarkable was birthed, a momentum for a second wind, or wave, of the prophetic movement that would honor and stand on the shoulders of those who had gone before, but will go into new territory with fresh understandings. I believe that this second wave will not always be compliant with the way things have previously been done.

HONORING THOSE WHO WENT AHEAD IN THE FIRST WAVE

Our prophetic leaders—our forefathers and mothers who have pioneered ahead of us—willingly, and quite remarkably, entered a fight that lasted decades for them, even to simply establish (or reestablish) prophecy, and the truth that believers can hear God's voice. Theirs is an eye-watering yet utterly brilliant and compelling story of "normalizing" the prophetic, against the odds and against all manner of opposition and obstacles. They had to be so super-focused on this work of breaking through, birthing, battling, and establishing that some of the issues we now need to address were left for this, the second wave generation. Each generation has their own responsibility, their own battles to fight, and their own level of glory-illumination to work under.

Prophets today must be always grateful for the lives of those on whose shoulders we stand. We rightly honor them, and nothing I write here should ever be taken as a criticism, usurping, or accusation against any individuals, least of all those spiritual mothers and fathers who have selflessly and generously raised me and my generation up and made a way for us. Given all that they have done, it would be unfair (and a dropping of our own responsibility) to lay any current shortcomings in the prophetic movement around the world at

> **Prophets today must be always grateful for the lives of those on whose shoulders we stand.**

their feet.[3] *This is a word to a movement, not against individuals or personalities!*

A New Purity Is Required

There is a new purity that is required in the prophetic, a higher standard to rid the movement of ego, marriage breakdown, weddedness to religious control or political spirits, and accidental oligarchical systems of leadership.[4] It is time for the prophetic movement to enter a fuller understanding of Jeremiah 1:10 and come to terms with what it means to tear down and build up.

> *Then the Lord reached out his hand and touched my mouth and said to me, "I have put my words in your mouth. See, today I appoint you over nations and kingdoms to uproot and tear down, to destroy and overthrow, to build and to plant"* (Jeremiah 1:9-10 NIV).

We cannot let strife, bitterness, division, competition, jealously, empire spirit, or insecurities go unchallenged. Nor can we leave the prophetic movement in the shallow waters of playing the game of "niceness." Equally we must not allow it to move into unsanctified criticism or unrepentance over its errors.

This second wave is a double-portion generation, which raises greater challenges for the prophet personally—because with increased anointing and authority comes great responsibility that requires deep, intimate character formation.

Be aware that it seems that the first and second wave leaders have slightly different emphases in their role before God. This means that it can be easy for them to inadvertently misunderstand each other's primary call and responsibility. We are in a live transition moment in these days, which necessitates much more than mere "succession and expansion planning" and requires a real contention for what God is asking His prophets to do right now.

Second Wave Prophets Are to Be an Echo of God

Our usefulness to God is based on the extent that we can echo Him. Authenticity comes from intimate replication, not independent prophetic assessment, of the divine! Therefore, we need to know what God is like in ever expanding ways, and not just the familiar ways that we may have met with Him in previous days.

> *Those who do wickedly against the covenant he shall corrupt with flattery; but the people who know their God shall be strong, and carry out great exploits* (Daniel 11:32 NKJV).

"The people who *know their God* shall be strong." It's one thing to ask, "How is my intimacy with God?" and a completely different thing to ask, "How freshly am I seeing God?" Be honest and acknowledge that knowing God is much more than you have seen to date. If I only see God in the ways that I have always seen Him over the years, with little growth, I cannot speak according to the breadth of His character.

Activation

Stop and seriously think about how you usually think of God.

- What are your three favorite characteristics of Him?
- What are you most comfortable with about His nature?

Take some time to write down some notes—words and phrases that come to mind.

SECOND WAVE PROPHETS REPRESENT GOD AS HE WANTS TO BE REPRESENTED

Most people who do this exercise with me will list a standard three: His love, His mercy, and His fathering are the most common responses. These are healthy, of course, but come on, prophets! We need to push ourselves further, to become happy with giving prophetic words that line up to more fully reflect the nature of the Lord as the God of the impossible, and which reflect a richer span of who Yahweh of the Bible truly is!

Over many conversations with other prophets, I have raised discussion questions with them like, "Should we hold back extreme words because it will bring wild disillusionment to the listener?" The type of conceptual conversations we have had among ourselves are along the lines of:

- "If we bring extreme words, will they just be too far away from where the people are at for them to actually hold?"

- "I'm concerned that people will just roll their eyes at me, or even stumble because they don't have faith for what is being said."

- "We know, but they don't know, the nature of God that He is putting on display! It will blow them up!"

- "What is the place of wisdom to temper my revelation here?"

> **Prophets must represent God as He wants to be represented, not as we think it would be best for Him to be represented.**

These are weighty questions indeed but, on the whole, I believe that we prophets must represent God as *He* wants to be represented, not as *we* think it would be best for Him to be represented in a particular situation.

SECOND WAVE PROPHETS SERVE AN EXTREME GOD

Earlier (Chapter 14) we saw that there is balancing tension in Heaven between two of the major characteristics of God: His goodness that saves versus His holy justice that corrects. Let's further lean into Scripture, beyond even these two extremes, to see what other fresh attributes of God we must be able to echo.

In the book of the prophet Jonah, we never read a word that he prophesies, but we do see that he has *not* reconciled himself to his prophet's call and to the extremes held in God. He will not go to speak against Nineveh because he does not believe they are worthy of saving. He will not bring a prophecy that gives the people of the city a way to repent and change, and so he ends up in the belly of the whale—just for not speaking what God had told him to! Jonah does not understand the depths of God's forgiveness and mercy and so he shuts his mouth. What is our lesson from this? We dare not speak (or refuse to speak, depending on the situation) on behalf of a God we have not bothered to understand the depths of. Are we far too familiar with the God we hardly know?[5]

If the prophet cannot continually learn about the nature of God, they will bring incompetent, inept words.

> *Yet you know me, Lord; you see me and test my thoughts about you* (Jeremiah 12:3 NIV).

God tests your thoughts about Him! He will put you in positions that are not comfortable to examine your mindset.

I still believe that abortion can be ended in our nation.

I still believe there is a great revival coming to this nation.

I still believe that the education system can teach the miracle of creation and a Creator.

I still believe we can live in a society that doesn't teach the sexual ideologies that are touted by the false prophets of our age.

I still believe that sex trafficking can be turned back and drug lords be put in prison because of righteous prophets speaking the will of God over a nation and prophets binding the principalities and powers behind the crimes.

I still believe that righteous men and women can arise in places like Hollywood and tell the stories of the fame of God.

I still believe men and women can rise to be the main people in government and politics, just like Daniel and Joseph.

If we *don't* believe these things are possible, we will never speak them. If we don't believe God can do all these things, the words will never come out of our mouths!

If I only see Him as father, I will not know what it is to meet Him as the spirit of burning (see Isaiah 4).

If I only see Him as friend, I will not know what it is to meet His kingly justice.

If I only see Him as serious, I will not meet His laughter or playfulness.

If I only see Him as the God who sits outside the circle of the earth on a throne (see Ezekiel 1:1), I will not meet Him as the loud, laboring woman in childbirth, panting, gasping, with engorged stomach, face knotted in agony about what is about to come forth (see Isaiah 42).[6]

There is a need for each of us to cry out for fresh intimacy with God, so that we might meet His vast expansiveness and be challenged by who He is—that His truth and His reality might meet my staleness and propel me into new life. Oh, that I might not "think" I know Him, and so repeat my stunted version of truth to others when there is a fresh ocean to be dived into of who He is!

How repetitive are the styles of your encounters? How diverse are your interactions with Him, truly? A.W. Tozer once wrote that, "What you believe about God is the most important thing about you."[7]

We have been called to speak in such a time as this.

We have to believe that what we say is stronger than the rebellion and demonic plans that stand against us!

We need the miracle-working power of God to move on our voice box and help us speak out again.

We need to break any agreement we have with the politically correct spirit that binds us from being bold in our words.

> **People are waiting for the prophets to speak of the justice of God, hungry for righteousness.**

I believe there is a nation waiting for prophets to stand in the gap again and declare, "Thus says the Lord, there will safety in the land for children again!"

I believe that the people are waiting for the prophets to speak of the justice of God, hungry for righteousness. They currently have no language to describe what they are pining for, but when they hear it, they will rejoice!

SECOND WAVE PROPHETS BRING STRONG CHALLENGE

The second wave of the prophetic movement will pick up the baton from our pioneering prophetic forebears, who had to wrestle simply to demonstrate that God speaks today, something that we are now able to take for granted (more or less!) in the church. The second wave will become more adept at strong prophetic words that echo the justice and judgment of God, the extreme emotions of God, and the passionate protection of His people.

People of revelation will outline the tough truths of sowing and reaping, or the serious consequences of national actions (whether blessing or curse). When Jonah learned how to echo God (even the portions of God he had not previously been comfortable with), judgment produced God's plan. (The judgment sentence of destruction wasn't carried out in the end, but the judgment word was a vitally necessary provocation to achieve the necessary result.) These types of "echo words" will bring about the holy provocations that even citywide, regional, and national situations require. God will use His prophets to further His plans for whole people groups, so that they ultimately might be walking justly with Him.

We all know from personal experience that we don't learn our key life lessons well amid blessings and times of lavish growth. Instead, we learn most in the pruning, clipping, and trimming times, and in the middle of wrestling, pain, and grief. If I were to ask you what was your major "learn" of the last year, or last five years, I expect that it will predominantly be something that you were taught because you faced a trial, a consequence, or a hardship. It is no different for our nations.

The problem with "God is good all the time" prophetic tendencies (in the way that *we* measure goodness) is that we forget the parallel rail track that keeps the Kingdom of God "train" in balance and on a straight path. Namely, that God is also fiery holiness, and that sin is deeply corrosive. Some of the so-called "challenging" things we have to say on occasion are really only challenging because we as church, society, and culture have strayed so far away from normal, biblical conversations that to fully echo God now seems like harshness instead of normal revelation! We have sat so long in the doctrine of the Father who brings comfort and ease (and nothing else) that we are ill-equipped to help people deal with hardship and suffering. We have an underdeveloped doctrine of the necessity of mirroring Jesus in suffering, or of being a repetitive echo that demonstrates the Lord's requirement for holy fire to consume all that is profane.

This second wave of prophets will echo God so closely that their words will break up hard ground. Second wave prophets will be instruments with teeth—not because they're difficult, rude, or cruel (God isn't), but because they're more representative of the full nature of Yahweh. They will more frequently release revelation publicly and privately that exposes, judges, *and* redeems. There will be shaking because of this, and much challenge to this type of prophet, who will rattle what has gone before.

PRAYER

> *Father God, make me a true echo of You and lead me into new sight of who You are. I desire fresh encounters that help me discover more about Your nature and characteristics. In Jesus' name, amen.*

ACTIVATION A

Open your Bible to Ezekiel 8. We're going to practice digging for revelation. My teams love doing this exercise! This Scripture takes us on a journey to push for deeper understanding in the middle of an intense encounter. Read the chapter carefully and then spend lots of time with these questions:

- What is Ezekiel's relationship with God like? Initially ignore the prophecy and what he is seeing and just look at and consider their interaction.

- How do they interact?

- How many times do you read either God saying, "look," or Ezekiel saying, "I looked."

"I dug and beheld" (verse 8)—do you see it? Ezekiel comes to the revelation like a spy, a secret agent, having to dig to see more!

He finds a hole, or window, too small for entrance, and is directed to enlarge it so that he can go in. Having done so, he finds a door that he is told to enter.

The object of this part of the vision is to show the extreme secrecy of what he is about to see. This should tell us that if we work relationally deeply, intimately with God, you can navigate further. God is inviting Ezekiel to dig with Him to see into the hearts of men and the ways of nations.

"Go in and see" (verse 9). Ezekiel is presented with the choice to go further. *"…So I went in."*

- Have you ever worked with God in the middle of revelation like this?

Verse 14—Ezekiel is now taken to another place of revelation because he has stewarded and worked with the previous revelation. Ask God to show you something, and then work with Him in digging deep to understand it, to see more. Watch how He rewards your persistence and desire for increased revelation!

There is a model here of dig, dig, dig… increased revelation… dig, dig, dig… increased revelation.

> *It is the glory of God to conceal a matter, but the glory of kings is to search out a matter* (Proverbs 25:2 NKJV).

ACTIVATION B

Now take some time to apply this biblical approach to prophesying over an individual. Ask God, "Show me the 'wall' that You want me to dig through to steward deeper revelation for this person."

CHAPTER 19

PROPHETS, NATIONS, AND PEOPLE

WHAT IS A prophet's responsibility to the nations? We've already looked at the fact that prophets spend more time in the business of hearing God's strategy for nations and groups of people, dealing with leaders, who in turn shape nations. There are five areas that prophets need to consider to ensure that they comprehensively guard and call nations into order:

FIVE RESPONSIBILITIES OF PROPHETS TO NATIONS

1. Establish the Future

Prophets call the *future* of nations to be established, forth-telling and commanding their destiny, according to what God wants that nation to become. This secures and holds the nation's future. We can inadvertently get into so much of a strong focus on the present that we forget how to protect the nation, prophetically shaping what it is to become for multiple generations. *What prophetic words are holding your nation's future?*

Top tip: Ask God, "What are You excited about for the *future* of this land?"

2. *Raise Up an Occupying Army*

Prophets have a responsibility to call the church into place and to raise up an army to pray, fight, engage, and occupy. This is a *present*-day focus in which the prophet leans into their Ephesians 4 role as foundational for the building of the church.

Top tip: Ask God, "What does the church need to know *today*? What is the truth You want them to be established in?"

3. *Welcome in What God Wants Now*

Utilizing the sight of the watchman, a prophet standing on the walls of a nation should be able to open the gates of a nation so that God and His Kingdom purposes may come in. "*On earth as it is in Heaven!*" This again has a *present*-day focus on welcoming what God wants now. These words bring explanation to what is happening in "real time," where we understand the season of God and why things are going as they are in the nation(s) right now.

Top tip: Ask God, "What is happening (what are You doing) in my nation *today*?"

4. *Set Nations Free from Their Past*

Prophets must also be able to set nations free from their *pasts*, and thus must be able to accurately identify and confront spiritual strongholds. This necessitates an ability to see where a nation has specific "open doors" (because of past sins and idolatries) to principalities and powers and may include the need to map out the territory spiritually, take the lead in identificational repentance, and tear down thrones, sin structures, and demonic ideologies. This is the prophet in high warfare mode!

Top tip: Ask God, "What is the top demonic force suppressing my nation, and how did it get into place?"

5. Expose Demonic Plans for the Future

Prophets should be able to expose hidden demonic strategies that the enemy has set as *future* "traps," thus setting the nation free to walk into its future. Here we move into the territory of knowing the "wiles of the enemy" ("the devil's schemes"—Ephesians 6:11). Again, this is the prophet in watchman mode, aware of that which will undermine our future well-being.

Top tip: Ask God, "Would You put me up on the wall of the nation and give me an alertness and understanding of satan's future plans by the revelation and insight of Your Holy Spirit?"

Generally, we are more familiar with words that talk to the church *today*, and most of us will be familiar with identificational repentance regarding our predecessors' sins from our nation's history.

> **Prophets have a responsibility for the past, present, and future of nations: prophesying, raising up armies, opening gates, liberating, and exposing.**

However, on the whole we have been much less clear about putting "today" into prophetic context, securing the future of the nation, and taking future demons out of action before they can strike.

Activation

Therefore, stretch yourself to write prophetic words that cover these five areas. This will bring you into the balance of hope for the future, understanding in the present, repentance for the past, and warfare that liberates.

The Role of the Prophets—Diving Deeper

Covenant Watchdogs

By now we should have a fairly robust, foundational understanding of a prophet's responsibility, how they sound, and what their role is. Now let us dive deeper together in our understanding of their duties before God.

Prophets are "covenant watchdogs,"[1] meaning that prophets come along in the Bible whenever God has made a covenant with the people. The biblical books of the prophets only make sense if we understand that they are guarding covenant—guarding the promises between God and His people, guarding the relationship of commitment. They are sentries over the binding agreement that God would be their/our God, and they/we would be His people.[2]

> **Prophets are covenant watchdogs, guarding the partnership arrangement between God and His people.**

Prophets guard the partnership arrangement, sort of like looking after a couple's marriage vows. No wonder they can be annoying! How would you like someone standing over your shoulder, commenting on how you are doing with your marriage vows every day? God is in the business of entering into intimate partnership with humans, and His prophets protect this.

Moses guards the covenant made at Mount Sinai in which, in Exodus 19, the nation of Israel is supposed to become a *"kingdom of priests and a holy nation"* (Exodus 19:6 NIV), put on display to all the surrounding nations. Therefore, the Israelites must be faithful, live by the terms of the covenant, and display a new form of humanity to the rest of the world. In essence, Prophet Moses, in leading and looking after Israel, will enable them to be a bright sign for other nations, calling them all to come back to the Garden of Eden, the dwelling place of God, where He walks with His people. God places His divine presence in their midst (in the Tabernacle, "Dwelling") and all they need to do is be faithful to the terms of the marriage (we call those marriage terms the "Law" or the "Mosaic Law" or the "Old Covenant").

God's Lawyers

So if the prophets represent God's interests in the keeping of the Law, we could say that they are lawyers, or "non-neutral marriage counsellors," working on behalf of God! A lot of what prophets say revolves around staying in the favor of God and therefore warning the people each time of how they might be close to breaking the terms of agreement with God that would push Him to call off His blessing over their lives.

The primary burden you will have as a prophet is as covenant watchdog, lawyer, and marriage counsellor. You represent the interests of *God*. (This means you are *with* the people, but not the *same* as the people—and you are supposed to offend and challenge current thinking when it is off course.) Priests/shepherds come in the opposite direction, as *representatives of the interests of the people*.

> **Lawyers (prophets) represent God's interests. Priests (shepherds) represent the interests of the people.**

Prophets, you work *outside* of the thinking of the institutional systems. You are *not* supposed to think the thoughts of those to the left and right of you! You fly above people, and churches, and nations, to see from God's perspective and what He thinks, always asking, "How does this look to Heaven?" as opposed to, "How does this look to me?" This is why throughout the Bible you find that God is in the habit of saying to His prophets, "Come up here!" In other words, remember who you are representing!

The Hebrew prophets of Scripture speak a bit like lawyers using poetry! They use ancient, arcane, covenant-lawsuit language, making arguments with legal terminology. If you are a covenant lawyer, the first thing you will do is point out what is wrong—naming, exposing, accusing. There are whole poems and speeches accusing people groups in Scripture. This flies in the face of perhaps what is a substandard approach to the prophetic today that always wants *harmony*. Never forget that to successfully outwork your prophetic function there is a need to frequently ask God, "How does this look from Your perspective?"

FIVE ACCUSATIONS PROPHETS BRING

The Bible's prophets have repeated accusations that they bring before leaders, nations, and peoples. You can see in the following five accusations what really matters to God, what are core values to our heavenly Father. As they are listed and we go through them below, have one ear tracking with the present-day international community of prophets. Are you hearing them speak along the lines of these biblical-standard templates? Consider the leaders you follow on social media and video channels—what would you say matters to God right now from how these modern-day prophets are communicating? Are they using a biblical template?

1. You Broke the Covenant

Prophets tell the people, "You broke the covenant. You did not keep your end of the deal in honoring God, His ways, and His life standards for you." Apply this to your nation; how are its people, or the church in the land, breaking or ignoring any covenant or commitment with God?

2. You Are Worshipping Other Gods

This accusation is often couched in marriage terminology in which the prophet describes the nation as committing adultery. Where and in what ways is your nation in unfaithful adultery toward God? What are the national idols that have been erected in place of Him?

3. You Have Allowed Injustice

"You have allowed injustice." The treatment of the poor, widows, and orphans is a very, very big deal to God. It is a key barometer for how well you are doing before God as a nation. Do you have the right advocate for the least and the littlest in your society? What is your policy for the poor? Letting the poor suffer and be taken advantage of is a key focus of the biblical prophets. What issues could you point to today that are riddled with national injustice?

Hopefully those first three accusations were fairly obvious and hence need no further explanation. The final two accusations are worth expanding on and exploring in more detail.

4. Watch Your Military Alliances

Watch how you form military alliances with other nations. This was a massive issue for the people who were supposed to be in covenant with God. How we align with other nations matters deeply to God. For Israel, God rescued them from the power of a military machine when they were in captivity and did not want them to be part of one again. Neither did He want them to support nations that used military might to oppress.

It seems that every nation today wants to become a mighty military power. If this is not carefully navigated in conversation with the prophets, it tends to lead us to make our nation its own god—we take care of ourselves and everyone else around the globe is left to fend for themselves. Do we know any nations like that?

In the New Covenant, God has called His people in and across the nations to ultimately be a kingdom of priests, which means that we get to minister to God and host His presence.

> *But you are a chosen people, a royal priesthood, a holy nation, God's special possession* (1 Peter 2:9 NIV).

How does a nation become a "holy nation"? It becomes a royal priesthood, it hosts the presence of God, ministers to God—and *God guards it* as His possession.[3] The Lord had His prophets tell nations to not amass huge wealth, not to build massive armies, and not to arrange lots of political marriages. Yet these are the three things our modern countries seem desperate to aim at. We, the modern prophets, have failed to lead the nations into dependency on God, understanding Him as our protector and provider, and working from a Spirit-led standpoint on all these issues.

Our nations have fallen far from the ideals of the Kingdom of God. No earthly government has ever fully looked like Jesus and His Kingdom. No lawmakers have ever turned the other cheek and then enshrined *that* as a policy for national behavior! No political party has ever turned and healed its enemies, blessing those on the other side who curse them. No nation has returned evil with good or lent money to their enemies expecting nothing in return.

In fact, we think this is weak.

Our manifestation of the Kingdom has become polluted to be much more domineering, impatient, and self-serving. Satan's biggest play is to offer us the kingdoms of this world, just as he did to Jesus in the wilderness (see Luke 4)—and we have taken it. We have grabbed his offer to be big and influential, to be right, to be a consumerist, to own, to hate enemies, to be individually great, to have power over others; a spirit to conquer and domineer for Jesus Christ is all consuming.

Prophets, have we been the voice leading the people into dependence on God? Have we as prophets truly dealt with questions like:

- Who should my nation be aligned with?
- Which trade deals should my nation have?
- Which international agreements and organizations have the approval of God?
- Are we wrongly aligned, militarily, as a nation?

So many times in Scripture the prophets are called in to answer questions of, "Will our war be blessed?" and, "Should we go to war?" Today's version of this question is, "Who is our enemy and who is our friend at a national level?" and, "Where should we wade in and help out; where should we stand back and not assist?" Prophets, don't assume anything! And be super careful to guard against *your* preferences, biases, and prejudices coming to the fore if you are ever asked this question. It is so easy to default to human intel or presumption.

Isaiah 20 gives us great instruction in how to approach these issues. In these six verses, we find out that the Assyrians are going to be God's instruments to bring pain to the Israelites because of their sin. Assyria has a strategy: it is going to pick off all Israel's military allies, all the countries that she has been looking to for help, mainly Egypt and Cush. And Yahweh tells Isaiah to loosen the sackcloth from his body, take off his sandals, and go about naked and barefoot. Basically, "I want you to streak in the nude for three years as a symbol of what is going to happen to your so-called deliverers!"

To paraphrase: "Israel, you boasted in your partnership with other nations; you thought your partnerships were ones of blessing; you thought those other nations had your backs; you made defensive alliances with them; you relied on other nations and not Me; you formed partnerships to protect yourself that I never gave permission for; you thought your partnerships would stop you from being destroyed. Because of this you are about to be embarrassed and afraid." The words in the Hebrew of what God wanted to do to Israel reveal that they would be anxious, dejected, confounded and ashamed, shattered, dismayed, and broken.[4]

The Lord was not only willing to bring the nation to its knees, but he was using Isaiah's nakedness as a sign of what He would also do to Egypt and Cush, her partner nations. Egypt and Cush will be led into exile with their buttocks bared and they will be ashamed as well.

Bear in mind that Isaiah lived in the capital city, Jerusalem. He was around the movers, shakers, and influencers; he was not living somewhere on the back side of the desert. His backside was *very* visible (literally!). In a similar prophetic act, Ezekiel has to make a model of Jerusalem, like a macabre Lego construction, to show its coming destruction. Jon Collins has remarked that Ezekiel was acting like the "Banksy" of his day.[5] This was visibly chilling art, designed to make a culture wince. The point of both these examples is that Israel and Judah's prophets were highly visible in instructing their nations about what they and their leaders were doing and the problems of their alignments. God is not so interested in what is happening politically, but He *is* interested in aligning a nation back into its right place with Him.

Therefore, a word of advice to emerging prophets: when you prophesy, please try *not* to start by giving your commentary on a political situation. Instead, bring the underpinning word of the Lord that holds the nation and brings clarity on what God is doing rather than on what a politician or leader did, or did not, do in any given moment.

5. *How Do You Treat Immigrants and Foreigners*

The final accusation that God's lawyers, the biblical prophets, are repeatedly seen to bring before nations is a measurement of how it treats its immigrants. This stems from Israel's Exodus story— Yahweh, your God, is the one who rescued you from slavery. Once *you* were poor, mistreated foreigners, so if you want to be His people, don't ever treat foreigners, sojourners, and the poor badly.

We prophets must have something heavenly to say on policies around strangers[6] that exclude, shun, debilitate, and dehumanize people who are made in the image of God.

> *When a foreigner resides among you in your land, do not mistreat them. The foreigner residing among you must be treated as your native-born. Love them as*

yourself, for you were foreigners in Egypt. I am the Lord your God (Leviticus 19:33-34 NIV).

The New Testament picks up on the theme, and this time it hits very close to home:

Remember that at that time you were separate from Christ, excluded from citizenship in Israel and foreigners to the covenants of the promise, without hope and without God in the world. But now in Christ Jesus you who once were far away have been brought near by the blood of Christ (Ephesians 2:12-13 NIV).

Here Apostle Paul is pushing the thought, "Do you treat the foreigner as Jesus treated you when *you* were an alien?" God pulls the language of the foreigner through both Old and New Testament to show us how important it is to Him. The Lord is clear: don't oppress or burden foreigners.

Do not oppress a foreigner; you yourselves know how it feels to be foreigners, because you were foreigners in Egypt (Exodus 23:9 NIV).

In the Law, God set a high standard for how Israel was to treat foreigners with dignity within their community. They were to:

- Be treated equally under the law and included in festivals and celebrations (see Deuteronomy 16:14; 26:11).
- Cities of refuge were available for them (see Numbers 35:15).

- Some of the tithe collected by the priests was to be used to provide food for foreigners, widows, and orphans (see Deuteronomy 14:28-29).

- Farmers were instructed to leave the gleanings of their fields for the poor and the foreigner (see Leviticus 23:22).

- Foreigners were not to be deprived of justice (see Leviticus 19:34; 25:35).

I heard on the news today that over 27,000 migrants from North Africa and the Middle East have perished in the seas of Europe since 2014. Every one of us will have a different opinion and perhaps even a different solution to the myriad of immigration, migration, and refugee crises that our nations and continents are grappling with in our day. My job here is to urge you to hold on to your existing ideas a little less loosely and ask ourselves some truth questions, so that when we seek the Holy Spirit on a matter, we will hear Him more clearly. For example, have we fought more to close our borders rather than open our borders? Are we a voice for the dispossessed? Or do we encourage the pushing away of the foreigner? Have we been brave enough to truly seek the counsel of the Lord on these issues?

What matters to God must be what matters to us.

On many occasions we have to admit to ourselves that we have not been biblically familiar and literate enough (especially with the Old Testament) to understand our role, and so we prophesy more to our own ideology (and our inherited church culture) than to God's. There is a need for all of us to surrender to the priorities of Scripture, because what matters to God must be what matters to us.

ACTIVATION

We are under obligation to ask God better, Bible-based questions:

- Jesus, what are Your thoughts on the poor?
- Lord, what are Your thoughts on our national alignments?
- Father, as individuals and as the church, Your people, how are we doing with the covenants,[7] commitments, and promises with You?
- Where are our gaps, God? For example, how are we doing with our refugees, immigrants, strangers, and people who look or sound different from us?

You might find it useful to have a pivotally honest, and personal, moment when you privately list all your opinions on these subjects (and more) on paper, so that you become fully aware of your baseline position. Perhaps you've never considered some of these issues before but discover that you had a viewpoint after all—maybe inherited from a parent, influencer, schoolteacher, or a book. From a place of understanding your default approaches, you will be more equipped to surrender these to God and seek His face for His opinion.

PRAYER

Lord Jesus, I am sorry for where I prophesied my opinion as Your word. Please have mercy. Would You realign my insides, my thinking, so that my mind might become the mind of Christ. I choose to surrender my political persuasions and ideologies, so that I can be a purified revelatory voice. In Jesus' name, amen.

CHAPTER 20

BECOMING A SECOND
WAVE PROPHET

BY NOW I hope that you are asking the question, "How do I become a second wave prophet?"

- Purge yourself.
- Fast your idols—don't let them hold you.
- Untie yourself from satan's "kingdom."
- See satan's false values with a new clarity, so that you can expose them, tear them out, and speak against them.

Much of your life as a prophet is dedicated to speaking against the values of the kingdoms of this world and the kingdoms of darkness. You will be continually reminding people of the two value systems: the Kingdom of God versus the counterfeit "kingdom" of darkness. If you tolerate any of the values of the kingdom of this world, you will not be able to fully prophesy successfully with purity. Therefore, *second wave prophet*, God is calling you into a deeply transformed and stripped-back life!

Jesus wants to give you an ability to see, identify, and speak where the line is between the Kingdom of God and the kingdom of this world. Prophets must not be impressed by worldly greatness. We must never see prophets fawning over their proximity to political power. Look at faith leaders and see if their confession is "Jesus Christ is Lord," or if they have stumbled to say, "We have no king but Caesar." It is a day to refuse to be compromised prophets any longer because we were led by compromised leaders! Break away from those who carry a spirit of compromise and therefore are prophesying in order to back the world's order, whether they realize it or not. I believe God's desire is for us to separate out from the spirit of compromise that would otherwise become a coffin around the voice of the prophet.

> Prophets must not be impressed by worldly greatness. We must never see prophets fawning over their proximity to political power.

RIDICULE THE WORLD'S VALUES

Surprisingly often the prophets of Scripture mock the values of the world. For example, they ridicule the perceived superiority of men on horses:

> *Some trust in chariots and some in horses, but we trust in the name of the Lord our God* (Psalm 20:7 NIV).

As for Elijah, our bolder-than-bold prophet is seen using tools of irony, humor, and contempt:

> *About noontime Elijah began mocking them. "You'll have to shout louder," he scoffed, "for surely he [ba'al] is a god! Perhaps he is daydreaming, or is relieving himself. Or maybe he is away on a trip, or is asleep and needs to be wakened!"* (1 Kings 18:27 NLT)

In a moment of crisis and spiritual warfare there is, within the prophet, the ability to display fierce indignation and righteous scorn. We often think that we need to tone down God's message to be really respectful or super sensitive of where the people are, yet the prophets sometimes carry an acerbic tongue. This is deeply challenging for those of us who are used to loving the way a shepherd would love. Being on the receiving end of a prophet is continually like being under the knife of a surgeon who cuts, cutting between the Kingdom of God and the kingdom of darkness in our hearts.

In Isaiah we read his total repulsion for Babylon's idols:

> *Bel has bowed down, Nebo stoops over; their images are consigned to the beasts and the cattle. The things that you carry are burdensome, a load for the weary beast. They stooped over, they have bowed down together. They could not rescue the burden, but have themselves gone into captivity* (Isaiah 46:1-2 NASB95).

Likewise, Jeremiah holds nothing back when he absolutely goes for the uselessness of the man-made idols that gentile men put their hope in:

> *Hear the word which the Lord speaks to you, O house of Israel. Thus says the Lord, "Do not learn the way of the nations, and do not be terrified by the signs of the*

*heavens although the nations are terrified by them;
for the customs of the peoples are delusion; because it
is wood cut from the forest, the work of the hands of
a craftsman with a cutting tool. They decorate it with
silver and with gold; they fasten it with nails and with
hammers so that it will not totter. Like a scarecrow in
a cucumber field are they, and they cannot speak; they
must be carried, because they cannot walk! Do not fear
them, for they can do no harm, nor can they do any
good." There is none like You, O Lord; You are great,
and great is Your name in might* (Jeremiah 10:2-6
NASB95).

No better than scarecrows in a vegetable patch! These prophecies are scathing exposures of false gods, religions, and idols,
and they continually make sure to rightly elevate the majesty of
God as a contrast at every opportunity. Perhaps in modern, less
poetic language we would say, "See the weakness of what you
have allowed to sit on the throne of your life! See the futility of
that which you prize so highly!"

Jesus Christ, as described by Paul, follows in the pattern of
the Old Testament prophets, only this time He doesn't just use
words, He is the active fulfillment of the words.

*And having disarmed the powers and authorities, he
made a public spectacle of them, triumphing over them
by the cross* (Colossians 2:15 NIV).

Our Lord put the powers of darkness to visible, open shame.
He stripped them, made them weak, and rendered them incompetent so that all could see. Jesus displays, disgraces, and holds the

dark authorities up, exposing them for who they really are as an example to us all.

BEFORE YOU MOCK, BE HUMBLE

Two cautions are necessary here. First, always remember that our battle is not with flesh and blood! We are not cruelly fighting or making fun of people, even as we mock the futility of their sinful rebellion and expose the evil that corrupts and poisons them. Ultimately, we are pointing people toward the redemptive salvation that is only found in Jesus and the good news of His Kingdom.

> *For our struggle is not against flesh and blood, but against the rulers, against the powers, against the world forces of this darkness, against the spiritual forces of wickedness in the heavenly places* (Ephesians 6:12 NASB95).

Second, you can only mock nationalistic propaganda, for one example, or be anti-imperialism, as another, if you have already been humbly stripped of their ideology yourself. We cannot go up against something prophetically if it still has even a foothold in our life. Putting this another way, you can only deal with the church's errors of evangelicalism, and its associated individualism (or any other *ism*, for that matter![1]), if you have "pulled it out" of yourself first. We cannot point the finger at the futility of thinking that a body modification or "sex change" will bind spirits of rejection, if we are still partnering with an orphan spirit ourselves.

The slightly uncomfortable thought in this is that we are going to have to mock and expose some wrong dependencies that are very close to home—even in ourselves! By "stripped" and "pulled it out" I mean, of course, the true repentance that means a complete about-turn, a rewiring, a renewing of the mind by the Spirit of God.

Second wave prophet, God is calling you into a purged, fasted, stripped-back, and deeply transformed life. For what purpose? So that we can expose the demonic strongholds, the false gods, and the idols that we find littered throughout the kingdoms of this world. Be a challenge to those who preach and teach that salvation comes through independence! Why do we not mock and tear to shreds the ridiculous, blasphemous idea that the good news of the Kingdom speaks of a particular political system, party, leader, or economic system? Don't be afraid. God protects reputations; He raises up, and He brings low. He trains us to be content in plenty and in lack.

CHAPTER 21

How We Communicate Revelation

Promises and Conditions

Prophetic words are usually either completely a promise (in other words they mean that God will do a thing no matter what) or else they have a conditional element—God will do a thing, but only if you play your part.

Promises

A promise is where God will act sovereignly, no matter what else is going on. What is your favorite promise of God? Not your favorite *verse*, your favorite *promise!* Take a moment to think about what surefire truth you stand on, or what assurance you hold on to that He will definitely do something or that something will happen. Here are three that we probably all know well:

> *Never again will I curse the ground because of humans,*
> *even though every inclination of the human heart is*
> *evil from childhood* (Genesis 8:21 NIV).

When you pass through the waters, I will be with you; and when you pass through the rivers, they will not sweep over you. When you walk through the fire, you will not be burned; the flames will not set you ablaze (Isaiah 43:2 NIV).

"For I know the plans I have for you," declares the Lord, "plans to prosper you and not to harm you, plans to give you hope and a future" (Jeremiah 29:11 NIV).

Conditions

Now, consider your favorite condition of God. This is where He says that if you act, He'll do something in return. We have an action; God has a reaction. Here are three examples of conditions:

Come to me, all you who are weary and burdened, and I will give you rest. Take my yoke upon you and learn from me, for I am gentle and humble in heart, and you will find rest for your souls. For my yoke is easy and my burden is light (Matthew 11:28-30).

Do not be anxious about anything, but in every situation, by prayer and petition, with thanksgiving, present your requests to God. And the peace of God, which transcends all understanding, will guard your hearts and your minds in Christ Jesus (Philippians 4:6-7).

Trust in the Lord with all your heart and lean not on your own understanding; in all your ways submit to him, and he will make your paths straight (Proverbs 3:5-6).

As you release prophetic revelation, be aware which category your word fits into, and make it obvious to the recipient, so that they are fully empowered to respond. I expect that we will all have heard these things done both tremendously well and dreadfully badly! I once visited a church that didn't have any of their children in any part of the service *ever*. In fact, they didn't even have a children's program—the teenagers came to church and sat outside every week, with zero spiritual input. Through what I prophesied, God released a remarkable intention of wanting to deliver signs, wonders, miracles, and extreme visitations to that church—but the condition was that "*if you exclude your children, I will not bring My weighty presence here.*"

> **Prophetic words are usually either a promise or they are conditional.**

I have heard prophets say that there will not be "revival" in the United Kingdom until there has been the spilt blood of a Christian martyr. This is clearly a conditional prophecy,[1] and we are grateful for its clarity. It may not be a condition we like, but time will tell if it's accurate.

ACTIVATION

Find some people to practice on over the next few days. Ask God to give you a prophetic promise for one person, and to another, a prophetic condition. Learn how these feel and sound different to give.

SPONTANEOUS AND SCRIPTED

I heard a well-known prophet say that they never give spontaneous words, only ever scripted ones. A scripted word is pre-prepared, written down, and usually edited—even added to—to a lesser or greater degree. Are you more spontaneous or more scripted? Immediate or reflective—how do you prefer to prophesy?

When the gospels recount Jesus speaking to the religious leaders of His day, we often read that He spoke with the *scribes* and the Pharisees. A scribe's role and primary gift was to write things down. They were usually a person of learning. Scribes had knowledge of the law and could draft legal documents (contracts for marriage, divorce, loans, inheritance, mortgages, the sale of land, and so on). In New Testament times, it was common for every village to have at least one scribe.

The important place of scribes in Scripture is clear—they are up close and personal to the cutting-edge developments of the day. It's a category of job that we don't really have the equivalent of nowadays; perhaps "copy writer" comes close. What this means, unfortunately, is that today we don't have many detailed, archived catalogues of contemporary prophetic words that have been spoken over nations. We have books, like this one, looking at how we *become* the voice of God, but very few that hold the *voice* of God (prophetic words) only.

Jeremiah came into a scribe anointing when God told him:

> Take a scroll and write on it all the words that I have
> spoken to you against Israel and Judah and all the
> nations, from the day I spoke to you, from the days of
> Josiah until today. It may be that the house of Judah
> will hear all the disaster that I intend to do to them, so

> *that every one may turn from his evil way, and that*
> *I may forgive their iniquity and their sin* (Jeremiah
> 36:2-3 ESV).

Jeremiah had been around for twenty years and knew what he was doing. He had a massive body of work to record onto his scrolls. Most of the canonical prophets are essentially books of sermons, the "best of" highlights and lowlights of the prophet's life.

Each prophet who is active today can generate a lot of material over time, and their core themes emerge. What are the key prophetic themes of *your* life; what are the core messages that you are being asked to carry? Most of the larger books of the Bible prophets have been collected and collated thematically rather than chrono-logically. Isaiah speaks of passing on his material to his disciples, which implies that these well-established prophets had crews or tribes of people that they could commit their work to, and the disciples carried on treasuring and stewarding the truth each prophet had received after they had died.

> **What are the key prophetic themes of your life; what are the core messages that you are being asked to carry?**

Prophets, we should be looking for books of revelation, not just training courses, to come forth from us as our legacy! It is important to write key revelation down, and in doing so to honor what the Lord has given you. I believe good prophets leave great revelation; are we are lacking this tradition today?

The fifteen books of the prophets in the Bible speak to us of a written prophetic lineage, shaping for generations, carefully documenting revelation over the time span of decades. Our aim today should not be five minutes of fame on a social media platform—it is not about being famous. In all honesty, if you're doing things well as a prophet, you will most likely be *infamous* and that extreme reputation is much harder to bear. It is time to commit to steward revelation for the generations!

When the prophets wrote their sections of the Bible, it was not a case of God saying, "Hey, Ezekiel, grab a pen, here comes the download," or, "Wake up, Habakkuk, get your chisel out—and where did you leave your stone tablets anyway?" It was much more about lived experience over seasons of gestating, birthing, nurturing, maturing a message that burned in them as eccentric characters. They end up with a body of work that has been accumulated through pain, tears, suffering, persecution, and in fighting for a nation.

Sometimes the authors of the Old Testament had help, as in the case of Jeremiah, where it is written:

> *Then Jeremiah took another scroll and gave it to Baruch the scribe, the son of Neriah, who wrote on it at the dictation of Jeremiah all the words of the scroll that Jehoiakim king of Judah had burned in the fire. And many similar words were added to them* (Jeremiah 36:32 ESV).

Apparently, Jeremiah gets on OK with his first scrolls then, after the heartache of seeing all his hard work go up in smoke, he brings in a professional for the end of the chapter. *The Dictionary of New Testament Background* tells us a little more about Jeremiah's fascinating, brave helper:

> Baruch ben Neriah...was a scribe—a prominent social position in sixth-century Judah—whose service to the prophet went beyond what was traditionally expected of a scribe. Not only did Baruch assist Jeremiah by certifying land transactions and writing down his revelations, but Baruch also, at great personal and professional risk, read some of these revelations to King Jehoiakim, who summarily destroyed the material. Because of this involvement in writing Jeremiah's revelations and sermons, some scholars have suggested that Baruch was responsible for editing at least some portions of the biblical book of Jeremiah as we now have it.[2]

Baruch's brother Seraiah[3] was a minister in the king's court and perhaps could have helped him into a nice, easy job, but Baruch chose to dedicate himself to the thankless and often painful job of faithfully following Jeremiah through times of prison, murder plots, and defying the king.

There is an anointing to be released for written communication and authoring the *rhema* word of God. If you need a scribe, ask God to send you one. For those who know they are to write, I release a scribe anointing on you now, in Jesus' name!

ACTIVATION

Practice a spontaneous word for a person—find someone and ask to prophesy over them, allowing the flow of the Holy Spirit to course through you faster and faster.

Then, practice a scripted word for a person. Take time to sit with the Lord and write down what He's saying for that person.

CHAPTER 22

A Word of the Lord to Second Wave Prophets Now

AS WE CONSIDER the dynamics of a pure, bold second wave of prophets emerging, we cannot ignore what the Bible warns us about how the new prophetic messages that they—you—will carry might be received by some who have gone before. As I wrote in Chapter 18, when introducing the "Second Wave," these words are not a polemic against the prophets who have gone ahead and before of us. Once again, we honor those on whose shoulders we stand—I for one would not be here today without them.

Neither should the prophetic message here be taken as a *carte blanche* to be rebellious, usurp authority, or ignore good leadership structures in your life and your church life. Do not misuse, misapply, or misconstrue the following Scripture exegesis, or the words of this book in general as a stick to beat those who are more senior, mature, and experienced than you and me, for you do not know the journey and the battles that they have faced and won on our behalf. The important commandment, *"Honor your father and your mother, so that you may live long in the land the Lord your God is giving you"* (Exodus 20:12 NIV) must always be in the back of our minds.

WHEN SUCCESSION GOES WRONG

When it comes to conversations about legacy and succession within the prophetic movement, we cannot ignore one of the most challenging passages in the whole of the Bible, 1 Kings 13. It is the scripture that shows how it can all go horribly wrong. Let's unpack the text together:

> *By the word of the Lord a man of God came from Judah to Bethel, as Jeroboam was standing by the altar to make an offering. By the word of the Lord he cried out against the altar: "Altar, altar! This is what the Lord says: 'A son named Josiah will be born to the house of David. On you he will sacrifice the priests of the high places who make offerings here, and human bones will be burned on you.'" That same day the man of God gave a sign: "This is the sign the Lord has declared: The altar will be split apart and the ashes on it will be poured out"* (1 Kings 13:1-3 NIV).

A younger prophet, a "man of God," receives a word of the Lord and is sent across country to deliver it. The word is a biblically typical, strong, foretelling prophecy, coming against the idolatry of King Jeroboam who has set up idols in a high place. The prophet travels, bravely delivers the bold word (note that he virtually ignores the king in front of him, the false priest, and addresses the altar itself), and such is the power of God within him, he doesn't just speak the word, he delivers an action and the stone altar breaks in two!

> *When King Jeroboam heard what the man of God cried out against the altar at Bethel, he stretched out his hand from the altar and said, "Seize him!" But the hand he stretched out toward the man shriveled up, so that he could not pull it back. Also, the altar was split apart and its ashes poured out according to the sign given by the man of God by the word of the Lord* (1 Kings 13:4-5 NIV).

There are many questions to ask, including, "What on earth is a young prophet doing being sent to Bethel, one of the greatest centers of prophets, to prophesy? What has happened to the established prophets who live there?" It seems that the older generation of prophets, the leaders who have gone before, have *so* lost their ability to confront and deal with the issues of the day that a young outsider

The prophets had so lost their ability to confront and deal with the issues of the day that a young outsider had to be sent to clean things up.

has to be sent by God to clean things up.

The king, after having his arm healed by the prophet and having seen all that happened, invites the young prophet to come and eat with him.

> *Then the king said to the man of God, "Intercede with the Lord your God and pray for me that my hand may*

> *be restored." So the man of God interceded with the*
> *Lord, and the king's hand was restored and became as*
> *it was before.*
>
> *The king said to the man of God, "Come home with*
> *me for a meal, and I will give you a gift"* (1 Kings
> 13:6-7 NIV).

However, the young prophet tells him he has been forbidden by God to stop in Bethel or eat or drink there (a further sign that Yahweh has completely rejected the prophetic company there). With impressive presence of mind, righteous determination, and the bravery to offend the king, he refuses the invitation and leaves.

> *But the man of God answered the king, "Even if you*
> *were to give me half your possessions, I would not go*
> *with you, nor would I eat bread or drink water here.*
> *For I was commanded by the word of the Lord: 'You*
> *must not eat bread or drink water or return by the*
> *way you came.'" So he took another road and did not*
> *return by the way he had come to Bethel* (1 Kings
> 13:8-10 NIV).

Now, here comes the ugly twist. One of the older prophets in Bethel hears about all of this and goes searching for the man of God as he is leaving town. The older prophet is so "off" his revelatory game that he has to ask his sons where the young prophet is! He eventually finds the young prophet sitting under an oak tree. (The Bible never wastes a detail—this is a symbol of the strength assigned to the next generation of prophets.)

The old man tries to compel him to come home and eat and drink with him, but the young man refuses. After all, he is obeying the word of the Lord. Then the old prophet lies to get his way, "Oh don't worry, an *angel* said to me that you were to come back with me." (Do you hear the echoes of satan's, "Did God really say…?")

> *The old prophet answered, "I too am a prophet, as you are. And an angel said to me by the word of the Lord: 'Bring him back with you to your house so that he may eat bread and drink water.'" (But he was lying to him.) So the man of God returned with him and ate and drank in his house* (1 Kings 13:18-19 NIV).

The man of God is enticed to stumble by the older generation, not discerning the lies and control that sit beneath the seductive offer. And, probably with a desire to honor and respect the old man's reputation, the younger prophet wrongly complies. Once back at the old man's house, the senior prophet stops lying and finally starts to really prophesy.

> *You have defied the word of the Lord and have not kept the command the Lord your God gave you. You came back and ate bread and drank water in the place where he told you not to eat or drink. Therefore your body will not be buried in the tomb of your ancestors* (1 Kings 13:21-22 NIV).

The conclusion of the story is tragic. The young prophet leaves and is mauled to death by a lion. The old prophet, in great remorse for having caused the man of God's death, buries the young prophet in his own family grave.

The Lord is cautioning us from this passage, but there is a necessary respect and honor we *must* have for those who have gone before. I cannot write this enough: We stand on the shoulders of giants. We want to read this passage through our fingers, wincing as we go, in case we speak wrongly against those who precede us, be they individuals, groups, denominations, or traditions. I am always acutely conscious too that for some, both now and to come in the future, I have the potential to become the "old prophet" of this story to them. Nevertheless, the Bible has given us this passage as a warning that all prophets, young and old, must only bow the knee to God and not be seduced by what the compromisers of the previous generation want you to do for them if it goes against what the Lord has commanded.

There is a fresh, cutting edge that is coming to the prophetic, especially in dealing with some issues that have been left to slide. There has been, on occasion, in some places, a dropping of the baton by those compromisers who were in the "right place at the right time" but didn't effectively deal with what was sinful on their patch.

First Kings 13 is the cautionary tale of a jealous, "old wine" prophet who tries to tempt the "new wine" to tone it down—don't be so determined, don't be so strong, don't be such a challenge to the kings who are now in power. The choice we have as prophets is, will we bow to the ways of an old wineskin? Will we tone down our message to avoid offending sensibilities? Will we be shaped fully by the desire and orientations of another generation? Will we let *them, or the Lord,* dictate our path? Will we walk with their slackness, or will we hold firm to redemptive truth-telling, bold holiness, and zero compromise?

If there is rot growing at the core of the prophetic movement that wants to speak "*peace, peace*" (Jeremiah 6:14) and not deal with issues, if there is a reluctance in leaders to submit to processes that would sharpen them, then a new generation will be sent into their territory to bring a word of the Lord to clean up the growing canker. Therefore, be careful not to be a "yes man" to leaders who have lost their spiritual edge and have been compromised by the spirit of the age. Be careful to keep your guard up and not curry favor with leaders who have not maintained their areas of responsibility.

In Bethel, Israel, in 900 B.C. the desire of the old prophetic community to remain relevant to the new political and religious powers in town meant they had turned a blind eye to the corruption of those leaders. A political correctness and kowtowing to monarchy had rapidly diminished them into the most extreme form of abandonment of the Law covenant that they were supposed to be watching guard over.

> Be careful to keep your guard up and not curry favor with leaders who have not maintained their areas of responsibility.

I know this sounds like revolutionary talk, yet we have lost years being what someone else wanted rather than embracing a call to clean up. The holiness of the prophets and their bold truth-telling of what is on Heaven's agenda must not be compromised. There is a time when we are all the young prophet and there is the time when we all run the risk of becoming the old prophet. May each generation keep its sharpness and be blessed to fulfill its function!

But Much, Much Later...

There is a redemptive end to the terrible tale of 1 Kings 13. Three hundred years later, in 2 Kings 23, the grave of the young man of God is found and honored—*by the very king that he had prophesied would come!* If you have been following along with your Bible, you will have read that the young prophet gave a remarkable word of knowledge about a coming king called Josiah, who would finally tear down Bethel's false altar to idols.[1]

Centuries later, King Josiah stands at his grave blesses it. This young prophet, who was misled, mistreated, used, and spat out by those who should have protected him, had secured the kingdom by forth-telling the king who would turn things around. This man of God did more with a short, obedient, and bold word than many did with their whole lives. May we all be in this prophet's image and may our legacy of truth-telling hold the Kingdom in our nations well.

Activation

Grab a pen and paper and answer this question: "If I were ten times bolder, what would I be doing that I am not doing now?"

If you wrote anything down, release your fear to Jesus and ask Him to help you to walk into the fullness of what He has brought to your mind.

New Ways, New Leaders

> *How long will you waver, O unfaithful daughter?*
> *For Yahweh has created a new thing on the earth,*
> *a woman, she shelters* [go around, turnabout,
> turnaround][2] *a man* (Jeremiah 31:22 LEB).

A woman shall turn around a man. You can almost hear the patriarchal Bible translators groan in attempting to grapple with this verse. It is *so* out of the order of the day—that a female could reverse a situation and bring radical change! But what we need to know from it is not a gender comment, but rather that *some things will happen that are exceptional to the natural order*. God is asking some people who have been hidden to now turn some situations around. The one you don't currently see, the one who is currently following behind, will be given significant authority to turn around those in established hierarchical leadership. A different order is coming, a different way is coming, and a new structure and new way of doing things is being released.

We all like the words "*new thing*" and are happy to prophesy it, but it will force the prophets to ask questions that are less about the day-to-day and more about the turning of nations. God has no problem messing up your faulty or incomplete theology and your current order—and He will, as turnaround time is invoked by Him.

GOD IS IN A DISMANTLING SEASON

Currently the Lord is dismantling ungodly cultures and empires that have stood for years. We all happen to have front-row seats for this. We are in days of political extremism, when the middle ground has disappeared, and we are swimming in identity politics. God is dismantling cultures that offend Him. We are in cycles of death and birth right now—significant deaths and significant births.

Demonic strongmen of death are sitting in ascended places, decaying the morality of the nations and bringing death—death to financial integrity, death of relationships, death of conversation.

But the Lord says, "Where you have allowed My values to be decayed and rotten ones to stand, I will dismantle you." God says, "I will not just dismantle nations, I will dismantle church culture that offends Me. I will audit My church."

God is seeking that His emerging, new wave prophets would speak out the extreme ways that He is doing things. The glory He is sending you will be inconvenient and will demand much from you. You will have to be prepared to say inconvenient, uncomfortable things and rise up and turn some things around (even though you might feel like the least likely candidate, or the least prepared person! But just remember Moses!). There shall be a turning around and an overturning that you are being asked to participate in. This means that you are no longer waiting for hierarchical permission; rather, you are demonstrating the new. (This does not excuse us from being under authority, accountable, and working with the other recommendations for healthy prophets.)

Prayer

> *In the name of Jesus, I take the pain off you where you were overlooked and marginalized. I loose to you the permission to birth, to build, and to become established! Amen.*

Prophets with Power and Extreme Words

We are going to see revelation partner with power, just as Moses modeled, in which signs and wonders become part of the prophet's toolkit in a much greater measure.

Remember 2 Chronicles 20:20 that we quoted back in chapters 10 and 12? *"Believe the prophets and you will prosper."* This verse will take on increasing prominence in the days ahead. If you recall, on the eve of a great battle against an enemy army, the people of Judah are told by King Jehoshaphat that they must believe the prophets to avoid being wiped out.

Have you ever wondered why he was so sure to seek and trust prophecy? Two chapters earlier, Jehoshaphat had entered an unholy partnership with Ahab to fight at Ramoth Gilead. Micaiah the prophet warned them not to go, but the two kings chose to take the word of a crowd of "yes men"—king-pleasing, false prophets—instead. In the ensuing battle Ahab is killed, and the dogs lick his blood from the floor of his chariot. As they wash the chariot, prostitutes also bathe in it! Ahab finally learned his lesson and God spoke to King Jehoshaphat in the strongest terms afterward: "You have helped those who hate me." In effect, he is told, "Do you think that God will prefer you just because you are a king?"

Therefore, when Jehoshaphat finds himself facing another battle in chapter 20, he is super cautious this time to call a fast and seek the prophets; he does not want to repeat the horrendous outcome of his previous misappropriated war. This time God gives him, via a prophet, the most ridiculous strategy: go into battle and stand still and I will fight for you. After his last disaster, this is a real test of his obedience—and of the accuracy of the prophetic.

"Believe the prophets and you will prosper." You need this verse because God is giving extreme words to His prophets in extreme times. It is in the day of the outlandish prophecies and impossible words that we grab hold of a verse like this with both hands. Expect

God is giving extreme words to His prophets in extreme times.

ridiculous words, intense words to come forth from you, words that command the weather and set timings in nations. Expect God to test you in obedience in delivering them and for your life to have to model gradual increments of yielded-ness—"Will you say this strange thing? Will you say this impossible thing?"

BUILD NESTS OF PROPHETS

It is tragically common to find prophets either in "caves" or alone, thinking to themselves that, "This is how it will always be as a prophet." However, the Bible has a very different approach from this, assigning prophets into geographical areas to live together and function as schools, or families, of prophetic replication. The scriptural standard is that prophets relocate so that they can share the same space and live in coalesced groups.

We do not want the restoration of prophets to be simply in name only and without action and lifestyle. Therefore, I believe God is creating "nests" of prophetic people, just as we saw in the Old Testament, where schools of prophets and companies of prophets lived and worked together. He is gathering prophetic people together and will reestablish what has not been seen since Elijah.

> God is creating "nests" of prophetic people, where schools and companies of prophets live and work together.

At the end of his life, Elijah visited the companies of prophets in Bethel, Jericho, and the Jordan (see 2 Kings 2). It seems that his last act on earth was to secure the legacy of these "nests" of prophets in Israel. Samuel too had nests: in Ramah, where he lived, and Kiryat Yearim, where the Ark of the Covenant rested.

In these five named regions, prophets came together to live, prophesy, and to protect regions. These groups would have sharpened each other and would have likely shared "prophetic intel" to cover regions and steward with clarity.

WHAT HAPPENS IN A PROPHETIC NEST?

1. Prophetic Nests Look After Each Other

Second Kings 4:1-7 is the story of the widow who receives the miraculous provision of oil. She is destitute after having lost her husband, *who was a man from the company of the prophets.* Elisha uses his miraculous powers to secure her future—he looks after the whole family, even after the husband prophet's death. Prophetic nests will look after each other and provide for one another in lack. It can be all too common that when a prophet gets sick or comes into a season of grief, there is no provision for them—and then they are in danger of accidentally undermining all their hard-fought-for reputations by ministering when they are not up to it (because currently, if they don't itinerate, they don't eat). Nests will help to medicate this issue.

2. Networks of Prophetic Nests Support Each Other

> *My master has sent me to tell you that two young prophets from the hill country of Ephraim have just arrived. He would like 75 pounds of silver and two sets of clothing to give to them* (2 Kings 5:22 NLT).

This verse gives us a little insight into how, in Israel, prophets traveled from one nest to another in pairs. That Elisha's servant had in mind to request clothes and finances for them implies that there was some sort of mutual support infrastructure in operation.

Nests of prophets help other nests. There is a network, not the independent isolation of an inward-looking nest. Prophet-to-prophet aid would ensure that prophets across a nation are all taken care of physically. Wouldn't this be remarkable if we could step into it today?

3. Nests Are Multigenerationally Cutting-Edge

We find a nest of prophets building houses together in 2 Kings 6:1-7. One can picture the scene by the river: the nest has grown; they move on to fertile land as one people, all living together under the supervision of senior prophets. The first miracle in this new home of the prophets is the floating axe head. This is a sign of the passing on of the cutting edge to the next generation of prophets. There is growth and multigenerational blessing as part of their alignment with one another.

4. Nests Enable Spiritual Growth for All

The example of 2 Kings 9:1-13 is that senior prophets in the nest delegate very significant tasks to others. Even, for example, the anointing of Jehu as king. Imagine if the Archbishop of Canterbury had delegated the anointing of King Charles III to one of his junior vicars!

There is spiritual growth and enablement allowed for all in an atmosphere of replication. (It's a limitless Kingdom, after all!) In essence, you will get apostolic and prophetic cities with prophets who live there and don't just drop in for fly-by visits. This is important so that they can continually steward the word of the Lord for the city and region.

On this level of shared lives and replication we must remember to beware those who want to separate the prophets. When we looked at prophetic companies in Chapter 12 we considered the Obadiah spirit that separates prophets and leaves them unsharpened, vulnerable to Jezebel, discouraged, and depressed.

5. When the Nest of Prophets Is Abandoned, Disaster Strikes

Bethel means "house of God" or "place of God." This name spoke of worship and fellowship with God. There was also a school of the prophets in Bethel. Hosea, who ministered over one hundred years after Elisha, called this city *Bethaven*, "house of wickedness"—a name of shame. Sadly, when the prophetic nest was abandoned at Bethel, the city became anything but a center of worship!

> *The people who live in Samaria fear for the calf-idol of Beth Aven. Its people will mourn over it, and so will its idolatrous priests, those who had rejoiced over its splendor, because it is taken from them into exile* (Hosea 10:5 NIV).

Bethaven was so called by Hosea because of the idolatrous worship Jeroboam (we already met him at Bethel earlier in this chapter) had established there, in order to effect a complete separation between Israel and Judah. Out of his greed for power and his fear that Israel would go back to Jerusalem to worship, he established two new places of worship in the north, with golden calves as the symbol of worship: one at Bethel, the other at Dan. There was no functioning nest to deal with this iniquity. The covenant watchdogs had gone. Yes, some old prophets were there, like the old prophet of our last section, but they had stopped functioning as a collective and had allowed idolatry to overtake their territory.

Prayer

Jesus, would You release revelation and an ability to work together as prophetic schools? We cry out to You to receive an anointing to work together and to coalesce as You intended in prophetic company. In Jesus' name, amen.

God is calling. The door of invitation is open to the prophets to join Him in His council.

CONCLUSION

I am ashamed to think how easily we capitulate to badges and names, to large societies and dead institutions.
—RALPH WALDO EMERSON,
Self-Reliance (1840)

THE THRILLING JOY of knowing Jesus is rooted in His aliveness. Every other god is dead. Controlling religion and institutions are the tragic byproducts of mankind trying to take the relationship we should have with Jesus and putting strident, controlled boundaries all around it, enshrining methodology over movement, protection over advancing, and taking power over liberation.

WELCOME TO THE COUNCIL OF GOD

God pulls His prophets out of the rhythms of the structures of religion on the earth, and in Jeremiah 23 He offers them a front-row, relationally interactive seat at His council. This is a breathtaking invitation into the ruling chamber of Yahweh, hearing the business of His decision making. On behalf of the Lord, Jeremiah laments the absence of the prophets from this place:

If they had stood in my council, they would have proclaimed my words to my people and would have turned them from their evil ways and from their evil deeds (Jeremiah 23:22 NIV).

This family council[1] is the place where the real heavy lifting of heavenly decision making is debated. It is the gathering of the representatives of God, the magistrates of mighty authority—those who will act in His name. I believe that God is calling and waiting, with the door of invitation open, for the prophets to join Him in this place, into His intimate counsel. The fullness of Jeremiah 23 gives some indication of the purity of heart, removal of baggage, and the breaking with institutionalized practices and poor habits that are required to get through the door. God desires prophets to turn the world upside down with words that will move mountains and from hearts that are with Him!

This call has gone out to us, calling us home to His council, calling us to seats in the great assembly. You can feel the yearning of God to gather and appoint prophets! Don't miss the offer, "Would you like a seat?" To be with Him in His decision making, to have His words woven through our beings, and to hold what matters to Him above all things is sheer delight. God is calling you into a new level of proximity where He wants to reveal, *through you*, a new breed of prophet long lost from the earth.

DON'T BE INSTITUTIONALIZED

In Jeremiah's attack against bad prophetic practice, he gives us an acerbic list that helps us to understand that we can have problems that bar us from the council of God. I would summarize this as the "institutionalization of the prophets." Institutionalization is becoming so set in what we think a prophet should be that it requires a rescue mission to free you. Being institutionalized is where you become established in your practices, established in your customs, and then these systems of practices and beliefs are left unchallenged and unchallengeable. It is when whole movements become less able to think freshly or in a more radical way, the place of being bound by expectations. It is time to break the mold. We have spent years raging against religion, which is appropriate, but it is a shock to find we are

Beware! Institutionalization is rarely recognized by the institutionalized.

still constrained by it. Now we must recover the fullness of what it means to be a prophet.

How much are we like the kind of prophets that we read about in the Scripture, from the first book to the last? Which biblical prophet are you most like in a measurable way?

Or do we look like a version of a prophet that might be palatable to our modern evangelical church movement? Being institutionalized means that we have lived under the rules of the culture more than we have lived in the context of the word of God.

Do any of us feel institutionalized?

No, you rarely do!

Do I look and sound institutionalized? Do I burn with revelation the way Jeremiah did? What prophetic acts and signs could the people I influence point to in my life? What boldness in commanding weather systems or national ultimatums have I brought or stewarded and then been measured in? We all like to think that we are cutting-edge and pioneering; we like to think we've given our lives over fully, but in Scripture who am I really like? What model do I follow? What template do I live by? Do I live with institutionalized blind spots, which, by their very nature, are unseen and unnoticed be me?

YOU WILL BE A SIGN!

This is not only about "come up higher prophets"—this is a whole new ballpark! This new sort of second wave prophet that the Lord is calling to emerge and awake is much more of a sign than we have yet been. You are going to be a sign, a distinguishing indication and miracle that makes God known. You will be transcending the common and you will go beyond what is normal. You will be a sign that testifies to the truth. You will be a sign and you will speak signs. This new sort of prophet is much more of a wonder than we have yet been. You are going to be a wonder—arresting attention, eliciting reactions from onlookers, used as a sign to point to Jesus. This means that you will leave an effect on all who are witnesses—a groaning, burning, demonstration-orientated prophet who is not just a wordsmith but is a living, breathing statement of the power of God!

The Lord speaks over much of the prophetic movement and says:

> Shallow waters, shallow waters! This movement is
> still stuck in shallow waters. Break free, break free
> of your traditions, and enter into the biblical model.
> For I need you to come down the mountain like
> Samuel's company did, visible in your anointing,

that people may point and say, "There—that is a prophet." For I need you to have sat with Me, not just hearing Me over nations but making decisions with Me about nations, feeling My emotions for them, My heart for them.

Wake up and feel the ropes of institutionalization closer to your skin than you have previously seen and realized. You are not yet the wild prophets you should be. You have the fire of personality but not yet the full fire of revelation. I call you the "keep warm" prophets rather than the "burning alive" prophets.

PROPHETS MUST FEEL GOD'S EMOTIONS

The prophet's job is to make God audible, which does not only reveal God's will but also His inner life. To be a prophet is not simply to be an attuned or attentive ear but is to be in fellowship with the feelings of God—to be an in-tune heart. We can accidentally spend years asking God what He wants to say and not enough time asking Him how He feels. The prophet must be in communion with the divine consciousness through the Holy Spirit, to experience the heart and emotions of God. If you only hear God's voice but do not feel His emotions, you will prophesy too lightly and layer your desire and your heart intentions around the words. Immature, entry-level prophets get fixated on what God is saying; they fall at this first hurdle by then wrapping how they feel around the words they have heard. This lacks prophetic purity and is often why we switch off to many prophetic words. The words do not grab our attention because they do not reflect the emotional status of God.

Honestly, how many prophetic words have we listened to that we switched off during them? It's because they did not bear the emotional hallmarks of God, though the words themselves sounded plausible. Some words carry weight and others do not, because weight and authority are tied into the prophet's emotional understanding of God. It is in feeling God's *emotions* that you come to a greater awe of your prophetic call. You reflect His inner musings and machinations, not just His external words. Prophets, this is the greatest privilege of your life!

WE ARE MORE THAN OUR WORDS

Beware that the voice of God (prophecy) can sometimes, wrongly, become a substitute for God Himself. But the prophet is not simply a messenger from God, merely conveying some sort of people-pleasing, inspirational teaching. The overriding importance of the prophet is not only the content of their message but the nature of the encounters and experiences that they have with God.

Therefore, this—being a second wave prophet—is not about being a mere mouthpiece for words (or even about being ecstatically possessed, for that matter). It is about coming into sympathy with God's emotions, understanding the Father's deep concern for humanity, fellowshipping with the thought processes of Jesus, and then transmitting the Sprit's message.

Yahweh has continual and constant involvement in the human story; we are objects of God's emotional concern. He is emotionally involved in the earth—this must be your start point as a prophet. If *His* start point is relational, emotional care, then our start point must be relational, emotional connection with Him. Our heavenly Father is not detached. In fact, His is the most moved heart you will ever encounter. He is deeply affected by human deeds. The Lord suffers when human beings are hurt; therefore, I understand that when I hurt someone, I injure God. As prophets we should be totally gripped by the anguish that Jesus experiences, for example, in human trafficking—modern slavery.

The prophet must never become emotionally numb or disconnected. The prophet must never become callous and indifferent. The prophet must never believe that emotions are surplus to requirement. Justice to the prophet is not simply an idea—rather, it is a divine passion!

> He is emotionally involved in the earth—this must be your start point as a prophet.

When the prophet shuts down, belittles, or demeans righteous, emotional encounters with God, then they will speak from an indifferent heart and that will ensure that their authority dries up. (Therefore satan will always try to confuse the emotions of the prophet so that we see them as unhelpful. Don't dismiss your emotions!)

BECOME A REVELATORY EMOTIONAL CONNECTOR

Remember that Jeremiah describes the feeling of revelation as something burning him alive from the inside like fire (see Jeremiah 20:9), and Daniel has to lie down for a week after the weight and the intensity of feeling the revelation that he received (see Daniel 8:27). Have we become "revelatory machines," rather than revelatory emotional connectors? If we have, this will have led us fundamentally away from revelation that people have a respect for. We will be churning out revelation while dancing around a platform and, in doing so, will have trained people away from an awe and wonder of a holy God. Ask yourself, how often do you hear revelation that genuinely puts you on your knees? Prophets, how often do you deliver revelation from your knees?

> *While he was saying this to me, I bowed with my face toward the ground and was speechless. Then one who looked like a man touched my lips, and I opened my mouth and began to speak. I said to the one standing before me, "I am overcome with anguish because of the vision, my lord, and I feel very weak. How can I, your servant, talk with you, my lord? My strength is gone and I can hardly breathe"* (Daniel 10:15-17 NIV).

THE PROPHET'S RESPONSIBILITY

If there is a lack in the body of Christ for eating solid, meaty, scriptural truth, we would rightly point the finger at the caliber of the teacher.

If there is a lack in the body of Christ of nurture, discipleship, and people care, we would rightly point the finger at the caliber of the shepherd.

If there is a lack in the body of Christ for winning souls and having a fully activated, missionary DNA, we would rightly point the finger at the caliber of the evangelist.

Whose responsibility is it to bring the standard of holiness? In whose hands is the burden for modeling the reverential fear of the Lord? From whom do we learn what it is to tremble in stewarding God's words and His ways? From whom do we learn the high bar of visible purity and holiness? All of these are what the prophets bring!

Their portion in the body of Christ is the reminder of the holiness of God, the need to get right with Him, the utmost importance of fearing Him. Theirs are the words and the lifestyle demonstrations that show how you live in light of a holy God.

Could it be that the requirement for a revival of the holy, reverential fear of the Lord in the church is only needed because we who are closest to God as His representatives have nearly all stopped modeling this? There was no one to truly set the example of how you respond in the presence of God! We've heard His voice but not modeled His heart and therefore stopped reflecting exactly who He was.

> **If the body of Christ is missing holiness, reverential fear of the Lord, and a trembling in stewarding His words and ways, it is the prophet's responsibility.**

Our responsibility is not just to prophesy the need for a revival of the wholly reverential fear of the Lord, but to be a visible demonstration of it and then to prophesy *from* that place.

So when we hear or read God say that we are institutionalized, as in the word a few pages ago, we are institutionalized in a style of delivery of revelation that rarely brings reverential, holy fear into the room.

Perhaps that's why we can prophesy so much political error and get away with it—because there is not the measurement in the earth, the comparison with prophets who are fully established in the council of God. Prophecy is a much more *emotional* business than we have thought thus far.

Although some of us have already given much of our lives to revelation and to the prophetic movement, this is a time, despite all our best work that has gone before, to come into a deep, churning repentance. It is not just about birthing the new and being happy that you think you are "new wine," because if we cannot unhook from the baggage of old traditions, we will ultimately replicate the past.

And so, we cry out to the Lord God Almighty that He would release grace for us to change and to become the emerging second wave of the prophetic movement that He desires in the earth.

PRAYER

> *Jesus Christ, You are our King, and we ask that You would take the years of institutionalized construction off us and grab us by the hand. Lead us in the biblical model of what it means to become Your voice. Amen.*

NOTES

CHAPTER 1 WHAT IS A PROPHET?

1. This is a parallel echo of Ezekiel's commission in the Old Testament, as a prophet to a "rebellious nation" (Ezekiel 2:3). In fact, John repeats Ezekiel's action and takes the scroll.

CHAPTER 3 PROPHETS AND THE FIVEFOLD MINISTRY

1. Geoffrey W. Bromley, *The International Standard Bible Encyclopedia, Revised.*
2. "The era of the church split" is something that I and others have prophesied about frequently in broadcasts and on platforms during 2022-23.

CHAPTER 4 PROPHETS AND THE CHURCH

1. This is an extended paraphrase of Proverbs 14:4 (ESV): *"Where there are no oxen, the manger is clean, but abundant crops come by the strength of the ox."*

CHAPTER 5 PROPHETS AND BIBLICAL LEADERSHIP

1. We changed the name of the program to Raising Prophets after we were alerted to the fact that there is another ministry called Emerging Prophets based out of the USA. Truly God is doing a work across the world!
2. With the exception of Titus (see below), this list of locations and dates is from F.F. Bruce, "Paul the Apostle," ed. Geoffrey W. Bromiley, *The International Standard Bible Encyclopedia, Revised* (Wm. B. Eerdmans, 1979–1988), 699.
3. According to Rick Brannan, "Titus, Letter to," ed. John D. Barry et al., *The Lexham Bible Dictionary* (Bellingham, WA: Lexham Press, 2016) the date of the letter to Titus depends on one's view of authorship. The traditional date, associated with Pauline authorship, is AD 64–67 (Kelly,

Pastoral Epistles, 36). Those who argue that Paul did not write the letter typically date it after Paul's death, between AD 80 and 90 (Fiore, Pastoral Epistles, 19–20 and Quinn, Titus, 19). Some scholars favor a date as late as AD 100–115 (Harrison, Problem, 10–12).

4. From The Enchiridion of Epictetus, c.125.

5. Upton Sinclair, *I, Candidate for Governor: And How I Got Licked*, 1935

CHAPTER 6 BECOMING A PROPHET

1. I gave an example of this in my previous book, *The Prophetic Warrior*. Once when prophesying over a church member I heard the Lord say, "As a sign of the validity of this revelation, you will grow in height." The gentleman I was prophesying over was in his 50s and well past any physical growth spurts. However, within three months he had grown a full two and a half inches and had gone up a shoe size.

CHAPTER 7 WHAT ARE PROPHETS LIKE?

1. Rev. C.J. Ball, "2 Kings 1:8," *Ellicott's Commentary for English Readers*, BibleHub, https://biblehub.com/commentaries/ellicott/2_kings/1.htm.

2. Eugene H. Peterson, *Run with the Horses* (Downers Grove, IL: InterVarsity Press, 2019), 46-47.

CHAPTER 9 THE THREE WAYS OF REVELATION

1. Hebrew translation references are from James A. Swanson, *Lexham Research Lexicon of the Hebrew Bible and Dictionary of Biblical Languages with Semantic Domains: Hebrew* (Old Testament).

2. I first wrote about this naba flow in my book, *The Prophetic Warrior*.

3. If you are interested in finding out more about deliverance ministry, visit my website at www.emmafaithstark.com where you will find resources to help you learn, train, and grow.

4. Swanson, *Dictionary of Biblical Languages*.

5. *Britannica Dictionary*, s.v. "Watchman."

6. Darris McNeely, "The Role of A Watchman, Part 1," ucg.org, May 31, 2007, https://www.ucg.org/the-good-news/the-role-of-a -watchman-part-1-what-does-it-mean-for-you.

CHAPTER 10 UNDERSTANDING THE ROLE OF THE PROPHET

1. Jon Bright, Jeremiah, *Anchor Yale Bible Commentary*, 1965), lvi.

2. Martin Luther, qtd. in Gerhard von Rad, *Old Testament Theology*, Vol. 2 (New York: Harper & Row, 1965) 33, footnote 1.

3. The phrase in Deuteronomy 18:18 (NIV), *"and I will put my words in his* [the prophet's] *mouth. He will tell them everything I command him"* is *referenced again in the life of Jeremiah* (see Jeremiah 1:9; 5:14) and Jesus (see John 17:8). In Acts 3:22, Peter quotes the words of Moses to confirm that he believes Jesus was the ultimate fulfilment of Deuteronomy 18:18.

CHAPTER 11 PROPHESYING INTO STRUCTURES AND SYSTEMS

1. *"Prince of the power of the air"* (Ephesians 2:2 KJV, NKJV, NASB); *"commander of the powers in the unseen world"* (NLT); *"ruler of the power of the air"* (BSB); *"ruler who exercises authority over the lower heavens, the spirit now working in the disobedient"* (HCSB).

2. The Church of Scotland was and is a denomination organized along reformed, presbyterian, Calvinist principles. The Roman Catholic Church had been outlawed to only the outer fringes of the nation, the Episcopal Church of Scotland was small and restricted to the point of decline. Methodism did not really take off in Scotland like it did elsewhere in the British Isles. See https://en.wikipedia.org/wiki/ Scottish_religion_in_the_eighteenth_century.

3. To find out more about the Haldanes, my dear friend Michael Marcel has written and recorded a video about them at https://ukwells.org/films/ part-10-james-and-robert-haldanes and https://ukwells.org/revivalists/ james-haldane.

CHAPTER 12 THE MINDSET AND COMMUNITY OF A THRIVING PROPHET

1. Good spirits—a state of happiness or welfare. For the ancient Greeks, this was the best you could feel.

CHAPTER 13 DEALING WITH WOUNDING

1. It is quoted first on Jesus' visit to Nazareth after His baptism (Luke 4:24), then on His second visit (Matthew 13:57; Mark 6:4) to Nazareth. C.J. Ellicott's (ed.) *Commentary for English Readers* (1905) says, "John's reference to it (John 4:44) may have risen out of one or other of these two occasions, but it conveys the impression of the saying having been often on the lips of Jesus."

2. I use this terminology as a shorthand for looking down on a situation, in the Spirit and by the Spirit, as if from Heaven's perspective. You are looking, not solely through your own eyes, at a situation—past, present, or future—but instead your vision should be augmented by that of God's perspective. As always, this is a Holy Spirit-led exercise and is therefore not human "visualization." Nor is it "astral projection," which is something that witches do. (I have to add these disclaimers because sadly some people choose to willfully misquote or misrepresent me!)

CHAPTER 14 WRATH AND ANGER, LOVE AND MERCY

1. The word *wrath* is not commonly used these days. It is a similar word to anger but carries the weight of consequence (judgment) to it as well. However, we must remember that God's anger and wrath is not like ours, which is influenced by our sin. He is always perfectly just, is never out of control, and is patient and merciful beyond what we can conceive.

CHAPTER 15 PROPHETS AND RELATIONSHIPS

1. "In the Bible, obedience is generally framed in terms of the auditory and the visual. The primary Hebrew word is שָׁמַע (šāma, "hear")."—Magnum, et al., *Lexham Theological Workbook* (Lexham Press, 2022); "Listening: People are called upon to listen attentively to God's word, to his Son and also to words of wisdom. Christians must not only listen to God's word but also put it into practice. Those who refuse to listen to God's word or to correction are condemned."—Martin Manser, The *Dictionary of Bible Themes* (2021).
2. William Shakespeare, *Hamlet*, Act I, scene iii.

CHAPTER 16 WHAT MAKES A FALSE PROPHET?

1. Augustine of Hippo, *Confessions*, I, 1.
2. Based upon excerpts from A.W. Tozer, "For Pastors Only: Prayer of a Minor Prophet," Alliance Weekly, May 6, 1950, https://equippingsaints. com/2017/11/19/insight-a-w-tozer-and-the-prayer-of-a-minor-prophet.

CHAPTER 17 BECOMING A USEFUL VOICE

1. This is a paraphrase of something that was originally coined to describe the role of newspapers in society. But it is really fitting to the role of the prophet, don't you think?

CHAPTER 18 THE SECOND WAVE

1. Christian International marks the beginning of the modern prophetic movement as being October 1988; therefore, it was thirty years old when the prophetic word on this page is given.

2. I heard Dr. Tim Hamon give this message at CI's annual conference, Autumn 2018. Quotations are from his written version of the prophetic word, as published at https://jenniferleclaire.org/articles/tim-hamon-prophesies-second-wind-prophetic.

3. Furthermore, and for the avoidance of any doubt, in this chapter I am writing in broad brushstrokes to make a strong polemical point about the current state of the prophetic, especially in the Western church (with which I am most familiar). There is no doubt that there always have been, and still are, exceptions and they should not feel offended or "tarred by the same brush." Nevertheless, we all need to be provoked now and again, myself included.

4. An "oligarchy" (from the Ancient Greek word oligarkhia meaning "rule by few") is a power structure in which power rests with a small number of people ("oligarchs") who govern an organization or a country. The entry in Wikipedia distinguishes these people as having one or several characteristics, such as "nobility, fame, wealth, education, or corporate, religious, political, or military control." In 2015 former US President Jimmy Carter stated that the US is now "an oligarchy with unlimited political bribery" when a legal ruling effectively removed limits on donations to political candidates—paving the way for Wall Street to spend $2 billion trying to influence the 2016 US presidential election. Oligarchies, therefore, are by their nature open to nepotism, control, financial manipulation, political meddling, and so on—all characteristics of the spirit of Jezebel.

5. I've heard both Bobby Conner and Bill Johnson ask a similar question.

6. *"For a long time I have kept silent, I have been quiet and held myself back. But now, like a woman in childbirth, I cry out, I gasp and pant"* (Isaiah 42:14 NIV). In this remarkably vivid passage, Isaiah draws our attention to the breathing of God in labor, groaning over His children.

7. This is a slight paraphrase of A. W. Tozer, *The Knowledge of the Holy* (New York: HarperOne, 1961), 1.

Chapter 19 Prophets, Nations, and People

1. This is a phrase I think I first heard used in a podcast by Professor Tim Mackie of BibleProject *(How to Read the Bible,* episode 23), this episode and episode 24 influenced my thoughts around prophets guarding the covenant, the accusations prophets bring in this chapter.

2. *"I will walk among you and be your God, and you will be my people"* (Leviticus 26:12 NIV). This sentiment is repeated over and over again many times in the books of 2 Samuel, Jeremiah, Ezekiel, Hosea, Zechariah, 2 Corinthians, 1 Peter, and of course, Revelation 21:3.

3. Of course, when Peter refers to a holy nation, he means the church. There is no such thing as a modern country being "holy"; a nation state can't enter salvation en masse! However, the truth principle remains: if a nation hosts the presence of God, He will guard it, and the people in it will know relative peace.

4. *"And they shall be dismayed, and they shall be ashamed because of Cush, their hope, and because of Egypt, their pride"* (Isaiah 20:5 LEB). Hebrew definitions from *Enhanced Brown-Driver-Briggs Hebrew and English Lexicon* (Clarendon Press, 2022).

5. Banksy is an anonymous but famous graffiti artist who makes public social commentary through art in public spaces. This was mentioned by Jon Collins in the BibleProject podcast series, *How to Read the Bible,* episode 24.

6. Denise C. Koenig, writing for the Christian NGO, World Vision, says, "You won't find the term 'refugee' in the Bible. But the Word of God has plenty to say about people called 'strangers' and 'sojourners' or 'foreigners' in our translations. 'Strangers' and 'foreigners' refer to anybody who lived among the Jews but was from another ethnic group — no matter what category they might represent in today's terms. 'Sojourners' are people who are temporarily living in Israel or traveling through the country. We use many different terms today for what the Bible

calls strangers, foreigners, and sojourners…refugees, asylum seekers, internally displaced people, migrants, immigrants, stateless people." Koenig, "What does the Bible say about refugees and displaced people?" June 8, 2023, https://www.worldvision.org/refugees-news-stories/what-does-bible-say-about-refugees.

7. Fortunately for followers of Christ, the new, better covenant was made between the Son and the Father on our behalf. Unlike the Old, this covenant can't therefore be broken. Nevertheless, we must be faithful and call others to faithfulness to Christ.

CHAPTER 20 BECOMING A SECOND WAVE PROPHET

1. As I have discussed in my online broadcasts, all -isms are, in effect, idols, or signs that you are heading toward idolatry. When we put any mindset, worldview, set of doctrines, political system, economic theory, etc. on a pedestal, we exalt it. Prophets must be very wary of preferring any -ism over another!

CHAPTER 21 HOW WE COMMUNICATE REVELATION

1. Note that the condition in this case is more subtle to identify. It is not the obvious—i.e., that one of us is to go out and deliberately get ourselves killed, like a crazed, jihadist suicide martyr! Rather, the prophecy is saying that the conditions under which believers are prepared, ready, and willing to love not their lives even unto death will have to be in place in our hearts before a new awakening can truly spread through the lands.

2. Evans & Porter, *Dictionary of New Testament Background* (InterVarsity Press, 2022).

3. Bromiley, *The International Standard Bible Encyclopedia, Revised* (Eerdmans, 2022).

CHAPTER 22 A WORD OF THE LORD TO SECOND WAVE PROPHETS NOW

1. *"A son named Josiah will be born to the house of David. On* [this altar] *he will sacrifice the priests of the high places who make offerings here"* (1 Kings

13:2 NIV). This prophecy was given sometime around 920-910 B.C. during the evil reign of Jeroboam, the first king of the rebellious northern kingdom of Israel. Three hundred years later, Judah's last godly king, Josiah, was born. Crowned at the age of eight, "the goldy influences of Hilkiah the high priest and Huldah the prophetess produced positive results. Josiah became the last Judean monarch who sought to restore the worship of God. He worked hard to remove the pagan religious influences of his sinful predecessors… [and] initiated a purge of idolatry in the land" (Williams & Horton, *They Spoke From God: A Survey of the Old Testament* (Logion Press, 2021). You can read the account of Josiah tearing down the altar at Bethel, just as was prophesied in 2 Kings 23. This is not the main reason that we're studying this passage however.

2. *EBDB Hebrew and English Lexicon* (Clarendon Press, 2022).

CONCLUSION

1. Various Hebrew lexicons offer translations of *council* as "confiding council," "counsel," "a friendship characterized by social or emotional intimacy," "a body serving in an administrative or advisory capacity," "an assembly," "secret," "circle of confidants."

ABOUT EMMA STARK

Emma Stark is an Irish prophet, church and ministry leader, author, and broadcaster, known by many around the world for her popular online shows and podcasts such as *Power Hour*, *What the Prophets Say* and *At the Stark's Table*. She is a founder and core leader of the British Isles Council of Prophets and, with her husband, David, leads an international network called the Global Prophetic Alliance (GPA), which resources and equips thousands of individuals, families, leaders, and ministries to grow in the gifts of the Holy Spirit, especially prophecy.

GPA's HQ is a home for prophets and all who value revelation. Every year believers from all over the world travel to Glasgow, Scotland to hear from God, receive freedom, and be equipped as prophetic warriors. Emma has been running a program for emerging prophets with GPA since 2019, now known as the Raising Prophets Mentoring Course. Many of the alumni of this program now regularly minister at a regional or national level, and over 80 have launched a "prophetic nest."

A fourth-generation Bible teacher, Emma communicates with a rare clarity, humor, and Celtic boldness. She operates with authority and authenticity as she ministers around the world, giving clear and direct prophetic input to leaders, churches, ministries, and nations, equipping the body of Christ to better hear from God to apply His revelation to transform lives, communities, cities, and territories. Emma has written several books, including *The Prophetic Warrior*, *Lion Bites*, and *Freedom from Fear*, and has recorded several training e-courses, which are available to purchase online. Emma has three children and lives in Scotland with her husband, David, and her father, Pastor John Hansford.